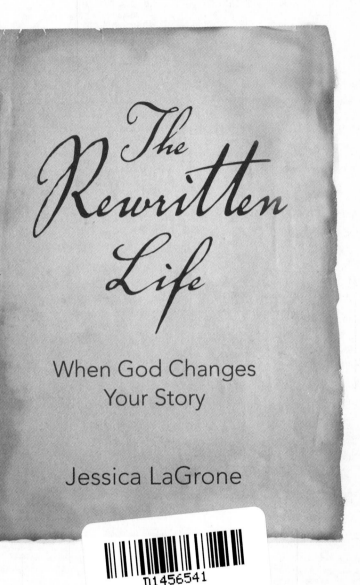

The Rewritten Life

When God Changes Your Story

Jessica LaGrone

Abingdon Press / Nashville

This book is printed on elemental chlorine-free paper.

Library of Congress Cataloging-in-Publication data has been requested.

ISBN 9781501834431

17 18 19 20 21 22 23 24 25 26 — 10 9 8 7 6 5 4 3 2 1
MANUFACTURED IN THE UNITED STATES OF AMERICA

CONTENTS

Introduction 5

1. Abraham and Sarah 11

2. Jacob and Esau 29

3. Naomi 47

4. Daniel 65

5. Peter 85

6. An Unnamed Woman 103

Closing Thoughts 123

Notes 127

Introduction

It was the first day of Freshman English Composition. We all trickled into the classroom, filling up the back rows first with the latecomers reluctantly taking seats in the front. Never the early bird, I ended up front and center. The professor breezed in and, with perfectly pronounced diction, presented the syllabus of assigned readings and an intimidating list of assignments for the semester. Once she was done, she asked us the first question of the class: "How many in here think they are already good writers?" Here was a question I could answer confidently! My hand shot up in the air. My grades in high school hadn't been perfect, but the one thing my teachers had praised again and again was my ability to tell a story on paper. With my hand still raised, I looked around to my right and left and then swiveled to see the rest of the room. Suddenly I was mortified. I was the only one with my hand raised!

That moment wasn't nearly as embarrassing as the following week when the professor handed us our first papers with grades at the top. Mine was a big, fat "C"! I had never seen one of those in an English class in my life. I was almost too humiliated to look the professor in the eyes. (Remember me—the only one crazy enough to proclaim myself a good writer on the first day!) When I turned to the page where she had written notes about how I could improve, I'll never forget her words: "It's not enough to write; you have to learn to rewrite too. Good writers are not born in the first draft but in the many rounds of editing, improving upon what they've written."

That advice proved helpful not only in English Composition but also in life. That year, and in many years to come, I would learn a hard lesson: I shouldn't allow my life to be a first draft. I often discovered that decisions I had made, words I had spoken, relationships I had blundered, and habits I had struggled to break left me disappointed in life and in myself. When it came to my dreams, I often felt that I was holding my hand high in the air only to have the results marked up with red pen and a grade that made me hang my head in shame.

What would I do when life wasn't easy? When my own efforts fell short? Would I settle for the first draft or dream and reach again? It soon became clear that even my own best efforts weren't the answer. I needed an editor, someone who could come alongside and take my first-draft life and help it become the masterpiece it was meant to be.

As I began to learn about the heart and character of God, I found a new kind of hope. The way in which I saw my first-draft life changed dramatically. You see, God is a masterful editor. When our stories need a rewrite, God is there with a new page and a new start. God knows the characters to send our way to shape our stories—the doors that need opening and closing. In the Book of Hebrews, Jesus is called the "author and perfecter" of our faith; he is perfecting our story and shaping us:

> let us run with endurance the race that is set
> before us, fixing our eyes on Jesus, the author
> and perfecter of faith, who for the joy set
> before Him endured the cross, despising the
> shame, and has sat down at the right hand of
> the throne of God.
>   (Hebrews 12:1b-2 NASB)

If God is the author, starting us off with big dreams and aspirations, then I'm grateful that God is also the perfecter, or editor, of our faith! God knows we won't ever get it right the first time and yet never gives up on our stories: "For I am confident of this very thing, that He who began a good work in you will perfect it until the day of Christ Jesus" (Philippians 1:6 NASB).

In the following chapters, we'll explore the stories of Abraham and Sarah, Jacob and Esau, Naomi, Daniel, Peter, and an unnamed woman, and we'll discover the transformational power of God through the stories of these biblical characters who came to know God and whose stories—and even their names—were never the same.

God wants to be just as intimately involved in *your* story, offering you an identity and a storyline that shine with the purpose for which you were created: to know God through God's Son, Jesus, and to become more and more like him, bringing God glory.

God has revealed himself to us in Scripture and desires to reveal himself personally to each and every one of us. God is a God who reveals and transforms. My prayer is that you will come to know God in a deeper and more personal way as you invite him to rewrite your own life story, allowing God's dreams for you to unfold on its pages. As you do, you are inviting God's transformation and responding to God's revelation.

Transformation is true and remarkable change. It's what happens when something is no longer its old self but becomes something else. All of the people we will encounter in our journey together experienced transformation at God's hands. God is not only great at creating (from scratch); God is great at transforming. When God's creation goes astray, God doesn't walk away in disgust. God "rolls up his sleeves" and gets down to the business of transformation. God nudges, whispers, shouts, pulls, and prompts until we get the picture of what God desires for us to become. And then God gently helps us get there. Through transformation God declares, "See, I am making all things new" (Revelation 21:5).

Revelation is more than just the name of the last book of the Bible. *Revelation* is the noun that happens when there is something to reveal. *Revelation* is what God does from beginning to end in Scripture. God reveals himself and his character to us in Scripture again and again, ultimately coming to us in human form through Jesus so that we might truly know him and how he feels about us. When we know who God is, our understanding of who we are and what we are about shifts dramatically. All true transformation starts with revelation, not about ourselves but about the One who has the power to show us who we are and change us into whom we are called to be. Through revelation God declares, "I AM WHO I AM" (Exodus 3:14).

Transformation and revelation are threads woven throughout the Bible and through our own stories as well. I pray these six stories from the Bible will help reveal for us six different times that God stepped into lives that needed changing and announced his transforming power with grace and truth. I hope you'll be listening for the echoes of your own story in each chapter.

After that first assignment in Freshman English Composition, I learned that it is never enough to turn in a first draft. I also found out that God wanted to walk with me and explore what it meant to live into the story he had given me. At every stage and in every experience of life we are led to ask again, "Who is God, and how is God rewriting my story?" May you discover more of God's transforming power as you get to know him as the author and editor of your life and faith!

Jessica LaGrone

Chapter One

ABRAHAM AND SARAH

*Then Abram fell on his face; and God said
to him, "As for me, this is my covenant with
you: You shall be the ancestor of a multitude
of nations. No longer shall your name be
Abram, but your name shall be Abraham; for
I have made you the ancestor of a multitude of
nations."...*

*God said to Abraham, "As for Sarai your wife,
you shall not call her Sarai, but Sarah shall be
her name. I will bless her, and moreover I will
give you a son by her. I will bless her, and she
shall give rise to nations; kings of peoples shall
come from her."*

(Genesis 17:3-5, 15-16)

Names Tell a Story

A name can function as a password, a key that allows you access to its owner. When I visit people in the hospital, that key can unlock doors or leave me standing out in the cold. When I walk into a hospital, the first person I meet is usually the receptionist at the information desk. My response to the question "Can I help you?" is generally to offer a name.

"I'm here to visit Mike Drummond," I said on a recent hospital visit. The woman paused, glanced at her computer screen, and smiled at me: "I'm sorry, we don't have a patient here by that name."

I'm used to this game. Because of privacy laws, hospitals won't give access to the room number of a patient unless the visitor knows the exact legal name entered in the records, so I tried again. "OK, how about *Michael* Drummond?" Same pause, back to the computer, and then another smiling response: "There's no one admitted in this hospital by that name." By this time I was beginning to get frustrated, but a few well-placed cell phone inquiries to mutual friends brought me back to the desk with my password ready: "*Thomas* Drummond!" I said triumphantly. Success! This time I was rewarded with a room number and directions to the elevators.

Mike lay in his hospital bed looking a bit weak but cheerful. Even cancer couldn't put a damper on his hearty personality. After asking about how he was feeling and when he might get to go home, I got to the question stirring my curiosity: "Mike, how is it that I've known you all this time and had no idea your name is really Thomas?" The story he shared was worth the trip *and* the delay in the lobby.

Thomas Philip Drummond Jr. was the first son to a wonderful mother and father. His dad, Tom, was proud to share his name with his little boy. The family lived in Illinois when he arrived but soon packed up and moved back home to be close to his mother's family. There was one little protest because this first-born grandson wasn't named after their father, his grandfather on his mother's side. Thomas Jr.'s parents insisted he keep the name he had received on his birth certificate, but the aunts would hear none of it. They began calling him after his grandfather anyway—Francis Marion Jennings, who went by Mike because he was too burly a guy to go by either Francis or Marion.

Thomas Jr.'s parents tried to stick to their guns but were overpowered as the whole family insisted on calling him Little Mike. Eventually even his parents gave in, and Little Mike it was. Mike claims that for the first three years of his life he thought his first name was all one word: Littlemike. It was a long time before he discovered his given name wasn't Mike at all.

Mike is honored to share the names of his father and grandfather. They were both honorable men, he says—capable, loving, strong, and family-oriented. He knows he couldn't go wrong being named after two wonderful men. He's proud to be their namesake—one given a name in hopes he or she will grow into that name and even that person's character.

Parents hope their little girl or boy will adopt his or her namesake's traits as the child is called by that name. Little Mike eventually dropped the "Little" and became just Mike. He hopes that he carries that name in a way that would make his grandfather proud. He also has great hopes and dreams for his own son, Thomas Philip Drummond III, who goes by Phil.

Oftentimes, our names are the starting point for telling people who we are. A lot of history is packed into our names, but names don't tell our whole story. In fact, sometimes we need a name change or a rewrite in our story. Thank goodness for a God who changes names and rewrites our stories, adding promises and blessings, and best of all—God's presence the whole way through.

Abram and Sarai

In Bible times, the way parents named children was definitely intended to tell a story—of who the parents wanted them to become, of the character or future hopes and dreams the parents had for them, or of what was happening in the family at the time they were born. Sometimes that got into some awkward territory!

In Hosea's family, the situation into which his children were born included their father's realization that he was not loved by their mother. Names for him and his unfaithful wife Gomer's children—such as "Unloved" and "Not Really My Son"—began to tell the story of a troubled family.

Abram and Sarai were given names that told the story of their parents' hopes for them, but they grew up to discover that the God they encountered had even bigger dreams for them—so big that their entire lives were about to change, including their names. God would do a complete rewrite of their future, and their identities would be so altered by God that their old names simply would not fit the persons they were to become. Their new names became a key to a new life, a password of sorts, given by a God who knew them even better than they knew themselves. A name in their day told a story about a person from the very beginning. If you asked someone, "What is your name?" you were saying, "Tell me your story; tell me who you are."

Abram and Sarai were certainly born to parents trying to tell a story with their children's names. Baby Abram was given a name that seems odd to us now. Not many of us would look at a tiny newborn, all squinty-eyed, with miniscule fingernails, and pronounce him "Exalted Father," which is what Abram's name means in Hebrew. To us, it seems strange to gaze at a newborn and call him "Father"; but to his parents it represented all of their greatest dreams for him. Abram's parents wanted his name to tell the story of his future life as one filled with prosperity, and for them that meant growing up to be a father with lots of children.

Without currency or stocks or investments, the measure of permanent wealth in that day was carried in your land and your children. So for baby Abram's parents to wish him a houseful of children who would exalt his name—calling him

"Exalted Father"—they were wishing a life of abundance on their baby boy.

On the day of her birth, little Exalted Father's future wife was given a name that's a bit easier for us to understand. Her parents looked at their little bundle of joy and named her "Princess," a term of endearment that we might use as a nickname today. Our Little Princess, they said, and in Hebrew that came out Sarai.

The Little Princess grew up to marry the Exalted Father, and even stranger than Abram's name must have sounded at birth was the irony that he grew up—grew old, even—and had no children at all. It must have been awkward for Abram to introduce himself to someone as Exalted Father and have to answer the inevitable question: "So…how many children do you have?" The Exalted Father was the father of none. He and his wife, Sarai, had been married so long that their friends had children—grandchildren even. But Abram and Sarai were childless. And in a culture that placed such high value on the number of offspring one had, this was a devastating blow.

Abram is seventy-five years old when we are first introduced to him and his wife (Genesis 12:4). And Sarai—well, let's just say she's no spring chick either. It's to these two seniors that God appears and begins to make outlandish and epic promises. From their first meeting in Genesis 12 and again in Genesis 17—where, by the way, we learn that Abram is ninety-nine years old—God promises that they will become the parents of many offspring. And in chapter 15, God gives Abram a powerful visual to go with this promise: "He brought him outside and said, 'Look toward heaven and count the stars, if you are able to count them.' Then he said to him, 'So shall your descendants be'" (Genesis 15:5).

In the time of Abram and Sarai, the stars were an even more meaningful spectacle than they are to us today. Without electricity or pollution, more stars were very visible in the night sky, and people spent more time gazing at them because there was little else to see after dark. The stars were a beautiful gallery of art, a map to guide their way, and a great and magnificent mystery. So when God promised Abram and Sarai offspring as numerous as the stars in Genesis 15:5, it was a mind-blowing prospect.

The promise of God's blessings in Abram and Sarai's lives would be so overwhelming that they would be utterly transformed by God. An encounter with the living God means that one's life will never be the same again. For our aging friends, their very identities would be so altered that it would be like two new persons had emerged. Everything would be different. Even their names would have to be changed.

Rewritten Names

Abram and Sarai may have given up hope that their dreams would ever arrive, but God hadn't given up on them. And once God took hold of their stories, they experienced a rewrite.

God's new name for Abram made it clear that the story Abram's parents had begun for him by naming him Exalted Father wasn't being forgotten but was being fulfilled. God changed Abram, Exalted Father, to Abraham, Father of Many Nations. With this new name, God strengthened the promise of blessing and offspring!

> *God said to him, "As for me, this is my*
> *covenant with you: You shall be the ancestor*
> *of a multitude of nations. No longer shall*
> *your name be Abram, but your name shall be*
> *Abraham; for I have made you the ancestor*
> *of a multitude of nations. I will make you*
> *exceedingly fruitful; and I will make nations*
> *of you, and kings shall come from you."*
> (Genesis 17:3b-6)

Instead of backing down on the promise in Abram's name, God put an exclamation point in it, making it stronger than ever.

God didn't forget about Sarai either. While her original name was a term of endearment meaning "our little princess," her new name, *Sarah*, carried with it strength, power, and royalty; it meant "A true princess, one who will be the mother of princes and kings." We hear the echo of this when God said to Abraham, "I will bless her, and moreoever I will give you a son by her. I will bless her, and she will give rise to nations; kings of peoples shall come from her" (Genesis 17:16).

Sarah's new name was close to her former one, but her new name was not just a term of endearment; it was a promise. God changed Abraham and Sarah's names from something that was just a hint—a wish that their parents had tried to put into words when they were born—to a promise, a reality that only God could fulfill.

Too often we underestimate the value of small changes God makes in our lives. What looks like merely the addition of one letter to us meant the world to Abraham and Sarah. Dramatic testimonies are inspiring, but if we miss the small changes God is making in our stories, we will miss the big picture God is painting for a big future.

**Too often we underestimate the value
of small changes God makes in our lives.**

A New Story of Worship

Their first encounter with God in Chapter 12 has Abram and Sarai humbled and in awe of the greatest power in the universe. Their response to hearing the life-changing promises that are to come is to build an altar and call on the name of the Lord:

> *The Lord appeared to Abram, and said, "To
> your offspring I will give this land." So he built
> there an altar to the Lord, who had appeared
> to him. From there he moved on to the hill
> country on the east of Bethel, and pitched his
> tent, with Bethel on the west and Ai on the*

east; and there he built an altar to the LORD
and invoked the name of the LORD.

(Genesis 12:7-8)

Building an altar implies both worship and sacrifice. Calling on the name of God means they are beginning to understand that the characteristics at the heart of God are central to the future they are now seeking. Even more than with other names in Scripture, the use of "name" in reference to God is so much more than a proper noun that can be spelled on paper or spoken aloud. It is a representation of the one who bears that name: of God's character, promises, and strength.

When Abram and Sarai call on the name of the Lord, it is about so much more than getting God's attention. They are worshiping and praising God for who God is and also looking forward to God's future help in their lives. At the beginning of Chapter 12, God approached them. Now they are coming to God, throwing themselves on the mercy of God's promises and strength.

When we call on God's name, we aren't saying, "God, do things my way"; we're saying, "God, in agreement with who you are, with all your power, love, and mercy, I call on your name—your character—to act in this situation."

Prayer that calls on God's name is not about hoping that God will come around to see things the way we do or that God will acquiesce to our will and do things our way. When we call on God's name, we are asking God to change our hearts, our character, to be more like God's—not the other way around.

Like Abram and Sarai, when we call on God's name, we are offering ourselves—our very lives—in worship.

The Rest of Their Rewritten Story

Abraham and Sarah's new names and the promises behind them sounded great; the only problem was that as time went on, it seemed more and more impossible they would see those promises fulfilled. It had seemed impossible when God first promised a whole country full of offspring to a childless seventy-five-year-old and his wife. But when God confirmed that promise by giving them new names, twenty-four years had passed. Abraham was about to turn one hundred, and Sarah was around ninety. God had promised them a people as numerous as the stars, but not even one child had arrived.

God sees impossibility as opportunities for blessings.

Their dream seemed like a lost cause. But God specializes in lost causes! God's favorite kind of story is the impossible one. The more impossible the better. God sees impossibility as opportunities for blessings. We need to know the impossible stories God has made possible. We need to be able to call the names of Abraham and Sarah because it doesn't always feel good when you're the one living the impossible story.

For years I held on to Abraham and Sarah's story and the promise of a God who could turn impossible stories around because I was in the middle of one myself. Neither my husband, Jim, nor I were approaching the senior citizen status of Abraham and Sarah, but we had been trying for some time to start the family we longed for. We had married a little later than most of our friends, and so we were eager to become parents. I had joked with Jim that I didn't want to have kids with an "old man" over forty, and so we definitely were going to have a baby by his fortieth birthday. But as much as I like to plan and predict life, as much as I like the satisfaction of putting things on a to-do list and crossing them off, that just wasn't something in my control.

Still, the sense of accomplishment was there when I walked into Jim's home office on his thirty-ninth birthday in my pajamas and held out a present for him. It wasn't wrapped; it wasn't even sanitary. It was a pregnancy test, and it was positive! Our feelings of joy and celebration were instantaneous; they were overwhelming, and they were short-lived. We were soon confronted with the fact that this baby wasn't going to make it. Our dreams had been dangled just beyond our reach and then snatched away from us.

Over the next couple of years, this was a scenario that would repeat itself again and again—the joy of discovering the hope of new life; the devastation of learning that we had miscarried as we stared into an ultrasound screen and waited for tiny heartbeats that weren't there. The emotional roller coaster of hope and devastation took its toll on me. I tried to pray, but sometimes I didn't feel like God was even listening anymore. I was devastated and angry, and I felt so alone.

But when I read Abraham and Sarah's story, at least I knew someone else out there had understood, had been where we were—in a frozen state of hoping and praying for something we weren't sure would ever happen. I needed to read their story to know that I was not alone. I needed to hear that a story like ours could have a happy ending.

Abraham and Sarah didn't have much experience with a God who made promises and kept them. The religion of their families had been one of polytheism—the belief in many gods. In this practice, their families would have had a shrine or altar with multiple idols dedicated to different gods. When they wanted something, they would pick an idol that specialized in that area (for example, a god or goddess of fertility, war, healing, or harvest) and make sacrifices and promises to win that god's approval and favor. Worshiping at the family altar was often about what they wanted and how to manipulate their false gods to get it, rather than responding to a god who wanted something from them.

This God, however, was clearly different than any they had ever heard of before. This God sought them out and made contact instead of waiting on them to do the seeking. God made promises to them that were about God's will—instead of them making promises and sacrifices in hopes that God would do their will. Most of all, God was real. And powerful. And loving. And more than capable of fulfilling every promise that God made.

Look how many times God uses the phrase *I will* in these verses of Abraham and Sarah's story:

When Abram was ninety-nine years old, the
LORD appeared to Abram, and said to him,
"I am God Almighty; walk before me, and
be blameless. And **I will** *make my covenant*
between me and you, and **will** *make you*
exceedingly numerous." Then Abram fell on
his face; and God said to him, "As for me,
this is my covenant with you: You shall be the
ancestor of a multitude of nations. No longer
shall your name be Abram, but your name
shall be Abraham; for I have made you the
ancestor of a multitude of nations. **I will** *make*
you exceedingly fruitful; **I will** *make nations*
of you, and kings shall come from you. **I will**
establish my covenant between me and you,
and your offspring after you throughout their
generations, for an everlasting covenant, to
be God to you and to your offspring after you.
And **I will** *give to you, and to your offspring*
after you, the land where you are now an
alien, all the land of Canaan, for a perpetual
holding; and **I will** *be their God."*
(Genesis 17:1-8, **emphasis added***)*

God was writing these promises into their story. The
promise that probably caught Abraham and Sarah's attention
most because it addressed a long-awaited desire of their
hearts was the promise of a family. God promised not only

a little bundle they could call their own but also a family that would be as plentiful as the stars in the heavens or the grains of sand on the seashore. This would result not only in a little nuclear family but also in a people, one that would be blessed by God and share God's blessings with the world. The "people" promised here were the beginning of a family line, God's chosen people. God promised to bring blessings to Abraham's offspring.

Actually, God promised Abraham and Sarah three things: the two greatest desires of their hearts—people and place and—a third thing they hadn't even imagined they could desire—God's presence. This was beyond what they could even imagine, because the presence of a God who loved and cared and guided them through life was unheard of. The greatest promise of all was that God would be with them, establishing a covenant to be their God and the God of their descendants. This third promise was worth more than the others combined. The greatest promise of all is God's presence—the commitment to walk with us as God's children.

While Abraham and Sarah were used to making their own promises to idols that were false and powerless, they suddenly found themselves in the presence of One who was powerful and true, One who took ownership of the outcome and made clear that he would be the power behind these great works by over and over again using the words "I will" to describe his intentions to fulfill this new covenant.

This God is clearly not one to be manipulated and controlled like an idol but is the one in control. The promises made are to fulfill God's will and purpose. As for an itinerary or timeline, God is not exact on that point. God simply points to a time in the future and says, "I will." I'm sure Abraham and Sarah were thrilled at the prospect of such great gifts arriving in their lives, while also wishing for a little more detail about how and when they would arrive. I can identify. I often wish God would spell out details about my future instead of expecting me to trust.

Letting God be in control is a hard thing, but the fulfillment of God's promises is so much better than looking to our own devices or fruitlessly worshiping the false gods of this world to try to get our desires met in our own timing. God's continual promise "I will" means that the responsibility and power for our lives lies in God's hands, not our own. If you'll look back closely at your own story, I'm sure you'll find it is marked by so many gifts that have already arrived: people who have brought you laughter, places that you've treasured, and most of all a presence—God's presence with you through it all.

God's Dream for Us

As powerful as parents' dreams are for their children, God's dreams for us are even more influential. They are the prevailing story spoken over our lives as we grow and become the persons God created us to be. Although Abraham and Sarah would forever be connected to the families that named them, they weren't afraid to step out of the path they were expected to follow and step into the plans of God. When we begin to ask questions about God's dreams for us, we may find an even greater story than the one we began the day the ink dried on our birth certificates. The God who gives new birth always has new plans for us, plans for a journey beyond anything we ever dared to dream.

The word *Christian* bears, at its heart, the name of Christ. When that name is bestowed on us, our story is rewritten. God hopes and dreams that we will grow to look like God's Son, to be like him in all that we are and do. The Christian's story is a complicated, lifelong process of transformation that begins with the simple act of trusting—and we can trust that God will keep on perfecting the story God is writing in us:

> *Let us run with endurance the race that is set*
> *before us, fixing our eyes on Jesus, the author*
> *and perfecter of faith, who for the joy set*
> *before Him endured the cross, despising the*
> *shame, and has sat down at the right hand of*
> *the throne of God.*
>
> *(Hebrews 12:1b-2, NASB)*

> *"For I know the plans I have for you," declares*
> *the* Lord, *"plans to prosper you and not*
> *to harm you, plans to give you hope and a*
> *future."*
>
> *(Jeremiah 29:11 NIV)*

Chapter Two

JACOB AND ESAU

Isaac prayed to the LORD for his wife, because she was barren; and the LORD granted his prayer, and his wife Rebekah conceived.

When her time to give birth was at hand, there were twins in her womb. The first came out red, all his body like a hairy mantle; so they named him Esau. Afterward his brother came out, with his hand grasping Esau's heel; so he was named Jacob.

(Genesis 25:21, 24-26)

In Need of a New Story

When I stepped off the plane in India, the sights I encountered took my breath away. The colors around me were vibrant, the smells intense, the heat, a sweltering 110 degrees

Fahrenheit. The poverty I witnessed was far beyond anything I had seen or imagined. Immense crowds of people clothed in dirt and rags, animals competing with beggars for scraps in the street, and the children—huge black eyes, unruly hair, mouths twitching at the corner as if they wished they could share a smile—they seemed to follow us everywhere we went. So many of them were begging on the streets, surrounding our mission group whenever we left the hotel and walking with us, holding out their hands. We were warned over and over not to give them anything because it would only draw more of a crowd, but my heart broke every time I saw their dirty, upturned palms.

A year later I came across an article online that brought that experience rushing back.[1] The phrase "renaming ceremony" caught my eye in the headline. I clicked on it and found pictures of faces just like the ones I remembered on the Indian streets.

The girls in the picture were lined up and dressed in their best, all 285 of them sharing the same name: *Nakusa*—a popular one given to girls in India, which means "Unwanted." In families overwhelmed by poverty, the birth of a daughter is seen as a burden, not a blessing. Her story begins with being unwanted. In the district where these girls live, there are only 881 girls for every 1,000 boys, a difference brought about by gender-selective abortions and neglect of baby girls to the point of death. Being unwanted is a life-threatening condition.

Concerned about the dangers facing young girls in their district, the government began furnishing free meals and education to families with girls. They even provided cash bonuses for families with girls who graduated from high school, a rare event in an area where education is usually reserved for boys. But in order to really change their stories, they would all need new names, so the government also organized a renaming ceremony for those named Nakusa and invited the girls to imagine a new future without the shame of being unwanted—to begin to dream a new story for their lives. These girls were reshaping their lives and choosing new futures by choosing new names. Some of the Nakusas wanted to be named after Bollywood stars, like Aishwarya. Others chose traditional names like Vaishali, which means "prosperous, beautiful, and good." One fifteen-year-old Nakusa chose to be renamed Ashmita, which means "very tough" or "rock hard" in Hindi.

A culture where girls are called "Unwanted" breaks my heart. But hundreds of girls writing a new story for their lives is a beautiful picture of hope. Just as their names and their stories were transformed, we are not doomed to be named by our pasts. No matter our backstories, God longs to rewrite our stories, to transform our circumstances. In God's eyes this is our story: we are God's treasure!

Jacob and Esau's Troubled Relationship

Jacob's story certainly started out on the wrong foot, with a name that he believed and lived out for many years. He hurt those he loved, stole what was not his, and ultimately had to flee for his life. But God had another plan and would set Jacob on a new course in life.

Jacob's parents, Rebekah and Isaac, must have felt as ill-prepared as any first-time parents. They had waited so long for these twin babies through the grueling journey of infertility. Rebekah's pregnancy was so difficult that she cried out to God, asking him what was going on within her (Genesis 25:22). Their firstborn was covered from head to toe in red hair, so they named him Hairy, which in Hebrew was *Esau*. Original, right? When they got really creative with a nickname, they called the kid *Edom*, or red. As Esau was born, they noticed that a little hand was tightly gripping his heel, as if to say, "Oh no you don't! I want to be first!" The new parents took one look at that little hand and named their baby Grabby, which to us is the name *Jacob*.

Perhaps more than in any other story in the Bible, Jacob's character was shaped from the beginning by his name. It not only reflected the circumstances of his birth, since he was grabbing at his brother's heel, but in some contexts Jacob also means "deceiver," "Taker of What is not His." This unfortunate connotation had a deep impact on the person Jacob would become. Most biblical names were given with one of two purposes: to mark the circumstances surrounding a person's birth or to describe specific character traits or gifts the child would grow to have. Jacob's name was both. His name started out as one that told the story of his birth—grabbing his brother 's heel—and ended up describing the character trait for which he was best known—grabbing what was not his. The double meaning of his name had unintentional consequences as Jacob grew into his name and its character.

When his twin brother, Esau, beat him to the finish line to be born first by a matter of minutes, Jacob's position for life was supposedly decided. As the second-born, Jacob would have inherited only a fraction of his parents' wealth, while Esau would receive a larger share called the birthright. Then, upon their father's death, Esau would receive the blessing as well, a spiritual inheritance on top of the final confirmation of the material one. This meant the elder would succeed the father as patriarch of the family and the younger would be subservient to his sibling as the ruler and owner of the estate as well as the spiritual leader. Being first definitely had its perks! This hierarchy certainly played a part in the conflict between the two brothers. There also were other factors that contributed to the discord.

Jacob wasn't going to settle for second. His name, innocently given as a reminder of his hand on his brother's tiny heel, could also mean "deceiver, supplanter, swindler"—one who grabs hold of what is not his own and takes it. And grab Jacob did. One day when he saw the chance to take advantage of his brother, he grabbed it. His older brother, Esau, was a hairy, ruddy, outdoorsy type. He came home famished from a long hunting trip to find that his irritating little brother, Jacob, had just dished himself up the last bowl of food in the house. Today we'd just grab some microwavable meal and the whole issue would be over in sixty seconds, but this was a day when the recipe for chicken nuggets would have started with the instructions "go in the backyard and kill a chicken." Preparing a meal could take all day, and Esau was hungry *now*.

Jacob milked the situation for all it was worth. He was younger, and younger children know that, generally, they can't win in strength, so they have to win in strategy. They have to devise a plan that is going to get them either beaten up or a really good trade.

Why would Esau settle for one bowl of food when someday he would own all the bowls in the house, not to mention the house itself? I'd like to look down my nose at Esau for his shortsightedness, but the truth is that instant gratification sometimes gets the best of all of us. At one time or another, we've all looked at something right in front of us that, if chosen, would mean serious long-term consequences, and cried out, "Go for it!" Short-term pleasure is gratifying, but long-term regrets can be shattering. We know they were for Esau. Have some stew. Lose your birthright. By no means a fair deal.

Jacob, too, experienced a gain and a loss in that moment. He gained exactly what he set out to grab in the first place. But what he lost was of great value as well. First, he lost a brother. They shared a womb and parents and a home, and now there was a rift that would take an act of God to repair. Jacob also lost any sense of goodness in himself as he surrendered to the dark side of his name. He spent the first half of his story struggling to take what was not rightfully his, and he would complete the plan and spend the second half of his life running away from the mistakes he had made.

> **What we fail to see when we grab what we want in the short term is that the relationships we overlook are worth far more in the long term.**

Jacob's epic struggle with the motivations within himself pulled him in two very different directions. His struggle raises an important question we must ask ourselves: *Do I grab on to things for my own gain while leaving my relationships in the dust?* There's a saying I love about the best rule to use when determining priorities: "People are more important than things." It seems simple, but that lesson is hard to learn when you're a small child whose brother or sister has a toy that you want. It's just as hard to learn when you're a grownup, hungry to fill some urge that will inevitably diminish a relationship that matters to you. What we fail to see when we grab what we want in the short term is that the relationships we overlook are worth far more in the long term. Learning to put relationships with others before personal gain is definitely not something that comes naturally. God urges us to break the easy pattern of putting ourselves first.

Ironically, I sometimes find these commands more difficult to keep toward the people who are closest to me—even family members. For some reason, their flaws and failings are harder for me to overlook than those of acquaintances.

As twins, Jacob and Esau had the closest possible of human connections. They also had the greatest temptation toward competition and contempt. The closer we are to the people in our lives, the more our familiarity can tempt us to treat them with disrespect. At the same time, our closeness can help us discover the amazing gifts God places in each individual. The relationships that are part of your everyday life have the potential to make you a jealous Jacob, or you can choose to celebrate the gift of your close relationships and the handiwork of God you find there.

I'll Be Happy When...

The rift between Jacob and Esau represents a struggle to be content. All of us have areas in our lives where we struggle to be content. And if we're not careful, our discontent will damage our relationships with the people around us, just as it did for Jacob and Esau.

Discontent also damages our relationship with God. A life spent wishing you had what someone else has shortchanges the life God intended you to live. When we become so focused on the blessings in other people's lives as Jacob did, we ignore our own and miss a chance to praise God for the blessings we've been given. We are basically saying to God, "I don't appreciate what you've given me or how you've created me. I'd rather switch lives with someone else."

Contentment doesn't come on like a light bulb when we flip a switch. It takes work and trust, and it is nurtured by worship, praise, and gratitude. These acts change our perspective. They help us focus on God's blessings in our own lives instead of looking over the fence at someone else's blessings; they help us treasure our own birthright and blessing instead of trading them away because we long for what is just out of reach. Knowing the limitless love of God means knowing there will always be more than enough to go around.

I'll be happy when.... Jacob seems to have lived by that motto. He grew up staring across the table at his brother, who was to receive the birthright and blessing, and dreaming of a day he could have them for himself. Riddled with envy and discontent, Jacob spent his childhood and early adulthood longing for what was not his and scheming how to get it. His attitude toward his brother and his parents was shadowed in a cloud of discontent and dishonesty. Jacob made the mistake of determining his happiness based on what his brother had. But our worth isn't determined by how we measure up against other people; it is determined by how God loves us.

Truthfully, Jacob had help developing this attitude. As with most family problems, the issues between Jacob and his brother, Esau, didn't just spring up out of nowhere. They had been brewing in the genes and behavior of this unusual family for generations. In fact, the ways that Isaac and Rebekah treated their boys contributed to the conflict between the brothers—with Isaac preferring Esau and Rebekah preferring Jacob.

Though Esau and Jacob must have felt special at times because of the preferential treatment they received, the favoritism shown to one of them no doubt was hurtful to the other. Whatever someone's reason for showing preferential treatment, it often communicates to us that we are not good enough, that we haven't earned the right to his or her love.

Jacob's chance to finally possess both the birthright and the blessing came when his father, Isaac, lay dying. Isaac knew he wanted to pass the blessing along to his older son, so he sent Esau out to hunt for and prepare a last meal. That's when Rebekah moved into manipulation mode, engaging Jacob in her plan of deceit that would ultimately divide their family.

Rebekah's plot involved preparing a meal, dressing Jacob in his brother's clothes that she happened to have ready for such an occasion, and putting goatskins on Jacob's hands and neck to cover his smooth skin. The story suggests this was a premeditated act she had been planning for some time as she schemed about how to steal from her older son to favor the younger.

When we share love, affection, and approval with another person, our storehouse is not depleted but multiplied.

Favoritism is the notion that in order to give a fuller measure of love to one person, we must neglect or deprive another. Judging from their actions, both Rebekah and Isaac believed this to be true, and they could not have been more wrong. Of all the commodities that families provide one another—shelter, food, quality time, love—love is the one resource that isn't ever limited or scarce. When we share love, affection, and approval with another person, our storehouse is not depleted but multiplied.

Families are sometimes programmed to act with a sense of scarcity, as if we have to choose who receives love and praise and blessing because they are in short supply. Our lack of contentment is often rooted in the feeling that we weren't given enough by our families of origin—enough love, praise, or attention.

Possibly the most heart-wrenching scene in this family story is a picture of Esau begging for approval and blessing, while his father believes there's no more to offer because he has already given it all away to the wrong son. Scarcity is the controlling idea on his side of the parenting equation, as well as his wife's.

The good news is that God never operates according to the principle of scarcity. There is no limit in how many prayers God can answer or how much love God can pour out. Just because God loves and blesses one of God's children doesn't mean God can't love and bless all the others. In fact, God knows specifically how to offer each of us answers to our unique needs. When we keep our eyes on the blessings other people seem to have, we lose the point of the contentment that comes from knowing our loving God provides all our needs.

When we, God's children, are behaving at our best, God showers us with love and blessings. And when we are at our worst, God *still* showers us with love and blessings. The idea that God favors one child over another is simply untrue. God's acts of abundance are in direct contrast with the world's belief in supply and demand. Unlike Jacob and Esau's parents, God is a divine Parent who is able to give with equal abundance, working for the best for each of us children, even when it's not apparent to us in the present.

Heading Home

When Jacob had the birthright and blessing he so badly wanted, he had to run away to hide from an angry Esau. Though he had the blessing, he no longer had a relationship with his family. So he set off to build his own life, to write his own story. Judging from the outside, Jacob was a success. He had a large family, livestock, and wealth. But on the inside, he was an absolute mess! In fact, most of his story was a tragedy of his own making. He spent his life grabbing at what was not his, poisoning the relationships that should have sustained him. Instead of being able to enjoy what he worked so immorally to gain, he ran from his mistakes, wrestling with an identity and a past that were toxic to him and to those he loved.

Even after many years of material success, Jacob was dissatisfied. Whether it was maturity, nostalgia, or regret, one day he began to miss what he had left behind enough to face the consequences of his actions and return to the scene of his crimes. He finally mustered the courage to gather up his entourage (which with multiple wives, a dozen children, and herds of livestock looked more like a traveling circus than a family road trip) and make the long trek back to his homeland. On the very last leg of his journey, Jacob learned that he was about to encounter the one person he needed to make amends with, his brother, Esau. The night before the confrontation, Jacob took everything he had accumulated—everything and everyone he had grabbed, deceived, or swindled to get—and sent them across a river called Jabbok, which means "emptying." Then he sat down alone. Finally, Jacob was by himself in the quiet to consider all that he had done with his life. It probably was the first time Jacob had been alone with his thoughts in a long time—only he wasn't alone for long.

Wrestling with God

That quiet moment led to an all-night wrestling match that was clearly a divine encounter. The authority this mysterious wrestling partner displays in renaming Jacob is the same authority that was displayed by God in renaming Jacob's grandparents. God showed up in person in Jacob's hour of need. That night forced Jacob to stop grasping at things and ambitions and grab hold of God. Still, Jacob was bold enough to ask his wrestling partner for a blessing.

The last time Jacob had asked for a blessing (from his father), he had lied, misrepresented himself, and taken on the identity of his brother. This time when Jacob asked for a blessing (from his heavenly Father), he was again asked in return, "What is your name?" His answer was both an introduction and a confession: "I am Jacob," he said truthfully. Deceiver. Swindler. Taker of what is not mine.

God knew it took a lot for Jacob to speak the truth at last. Even so, God wasn't satisfied with leaving Jacob as he was. God wants to hear our honest confession and assessment of who we are and where we find ourselves, but that doesn't mean God will leave us that way. Only when we are honest about our desperate state and our desperate need can God set about changing us to become the ones he wants us to be.

During that unbelievable wrestling match, Jacob tried all of his usual grabby tricks to get what he wanted. He demanded to know his opponent's name, which was a way of trying to grab victory, asking for power or control over the story. Even today we understand a little bit of the power of calling someone by name. Most of us have three names—a first, middle, and last. Who has the authority and power to call you by all three names? Usually it is only the ones who gave you those names, and usually they are exercising quite a bit of power and authority when they do! If you overhear me call my son "Andrew James LaGrone," you'd better believe some authority is about to go down.

So, when Jacob demanded to call God by name, he was adamantly turned down. No one controls God. Instead, God showed his power over Jacob by calling him by name, and in fact, changing that name.

> *"You shall no longer be called Jacob, but Israel, for you have striven with God and with humans, and have prevailed."*
>
> *(Genesis 32:28)*

Jacob went from being grabby, deceiver, one who takes selfishly, to *Israel*, one who wrestles with God. The people promised to Abraham and Sarah would now have a name, children of Israel—the ones who wrestle with God, who grab onto God in difficult times and hold on for dear life. At that moment, Jacob the deceiver no longer existed.

Soon after God's life-changing and name-changing meeting with Jacob, God began to identify himself as "The God of Abraham, Isaac, and Jacob." This divine introduction is an amazing occurrence, so don't miss the implications. The Holy God who created the universe began to introduce himself by naming the names of God's own people!

It's as if God was saying, "If you want to know who I am, check out what I did in the lives of these people. The changes I've accomplished in their stories will show you my power, my grace, my attentive care to their smallest and greatest needs." The changes in their lives authenticated the character of God, so God began to point them out as God's signature. God was saying, "I am best known through my handiwork—and you are my most significant handiwork!"

When I think of the fact that God wants to show God's character to the world through me and be called "The God of Jessica," knowing that people will recognize God's character in my life, it brings a whole new significance to my longing to be more like God. I want to be sure that people see the story of my life as one of God-sized transformation—a story in which names and words have incredible power, forming the "chapter titles" that shape our lives.

New Chapter Titles

In some families, children are shaped by beautiful, positive words that will help them grow in confidence. In others, they are scarred with words that will become the chapter titles of their childhood stories, words that brand them in ways they will struggle with for a very long time. If we're honest, most of our families have given us both.

I've watched a child in a tutoring program struggle over his homework, coming to a problem he could not answer and whispering to himself as he put his head down on the paper, "Stupid. Stupid. Stupid." That name came from someone, somewhere. And it stuck. I've seen my husband fumble and drop something in the kitchen and heard the first word that popped out of his mouth: "Clumsy!" I've struggled, too, looking in the mirror on those days when the skinny jeans just wouldn't fit. (OK, let's be honest, when the not-so-skinny jeans wouldn't fit either!) There are days, too, when the task I'm trying to accomplish seems beyond my abilities or comfort zone. In those moments the adjectives that popped into my head are names of sorts, things I was once called by peers or unwitting family members who never knew their words would stick and come to the surface later in life.

The truth is that our stories are shaped by the words spoken over us: words spoken by people who shower us with encouragement and admiration, and words spoken in careless moments of criticism. The reminder that we are also accountable for speaking words into the lives of the people we love is a sobering and sacred responsibility.

> **Our stories are shaped by the words spoken over us.... The reminder that we are also accountable for speaking words into the lives of the people we love is a sobering and sacred responsibility.**

The challenge in life is to sort out the titles given to the chapters of our lives. We need to recognize and accept the names we have been given that God nods and smiles at, ones given by people speaking with God's spirit and character. God definitely uses people as mouthpieces to push us forward in life to discover the identity that God has created for us. We also need to identify which names are ones that don't reflect God's vision and identity for us—harmful names spoken in haste or hate or anger, names that we will be better off allowing God to erase. For most of us, discovering and changing those titles will be a lifelong endeavor, but awareness is a crucial first step.

Jacob's story teaches us that words matter, no matter how small, and that getting what you want doesn't always bring you the happiness you expected. However, Jacob's story also shows us that no storyline is doomed if God wants to rewrite it. It doesn't matter where we are in our story; God always has the power to start us over on a transformed path, showering us with God's grace.

Chapter Three

NAOMI

But Naomi said, "Turn back, my daughters, why will you go with me? Do I still have sons in my womb that they may become your husbands? Turn back, my daughters, go your way, for I am too old to have a husband. Even if I thought there was hope for me, even if I should have a husband tonight and bear sons, would you then wait until they were grown? Would you then refrain from marrying? No, my daughters, it has been far more bitter for me than for you, because the hand of the Lord *has turned against me." Then they wept aloud again. Orpah kissed her mother-in-law, but Ruth clung to her.*

(Ruth 1:11-14)

Grief Changes Everything

Grief takes your breath away. My breathless moment is frozen in a memory in front of a Christmas tree at my grandmother's house. We were finishing up the last touches on decorations, presents, and dinner while waiting for my aunt and uncle and their four kids to arrive. The phone rang. My mom answered it, and I could tell it was her brother on the other line. I remember wondering why they were running late. Then I heard my mom say, "Oh, no. Oh, no," over and over again. And then finally: "Oh, I'm so sorry." My uncle and his family had arrived at their home to find their oldest son had taken his own life. He was just twenty years old.

Time stopped for me in those few seconds after the phone rang. I can remember with odd clarity the tiny details of the room, the ache and shock that I felt, and the immediate concern for my ninety-year-old grandmother, whom we'd break the news to within minutes. Our family faced a very different kind of Christmas that year, one with grief as a centerpiece, overshadowing all the plans we had made.

We often use the words "family members" to describe those who are related to us. The term *members* is also used to describe the parts of our body; arms and legs are members of a whole. When one member is badly hurt or even removed, the whole body goes into a kind of shock, feeling the pain of dismemberment. The same is true when those we love are taken away. Then shock and numbness give way to overwhelming pain.

Naomi's life was torn apart when she lost everything she knew and loved. In the very first verse of the Book of Ruth we learn that her homeland was rocked by such severe famine that her family was forced to evacuate, becoming refugees in the neighboring country of Moab. The first loss Naomi experienced was the loss of her livelihood—her own sustenance and her ability to feed her family. This led to the loss of her home, her friends, and the familiarity of all that she knew as she and her husband fled to another country with their two boys just to survive. If these were Naomi's only losses we would feel sorry for her, but they were nothing compared to the losses that were to come.

Next, Naomi lost the three most important people in her life—her husband and two sons. Her family was dismembered, torn apart. How did Naomi react? Not surprisingly, she was grief-stricken, bitter, and angry at God. Her daughters-in-law were loyal to her and wanted to stay with her, even though they were grieving the losses of their own husbands. But even with their attempts to comfort her, Naomi's reaction shows us how alone and dejected she felt. After she returned to Bethlehem, the women in the town were so surprised to see Naomi again. They exclaimed, "Can this be Naomi?" Naomi's response spoke volumes about her emotional state:

> *"Call me no longer Naomi,*
> *call me Mara,*
> *for the Almighty has dealt bitterly with me.*

I went away full,
but the LORD has brought me back empty;
why call me Naomi
when the LORD has dealt harshly with me,
and the Almighty has brought calamity
upon me?"

(Ruth 1:20-21)

With no one left to call her "*Honey*," no one left to call her "*Mom*," Naomi decided that "*bitter*" was the name that best applied to her story. She allowed the grief to take over and her story to become a tragedy. Naomi's reaction isn't that surprising, really. How can we blame her for holding God responsible for the avalanche of tragedies she endured? When there's no easy explanation or person to blame, God is often the target for our anger.

As with achieving intimacy in any healthy human relationship, we can't be truly close to God in good times unless we are truly transparent with God in bad times as well.

God wants to know our hearts and have us express ourselves honestly. As with achieving intimacy in any healthy human relationship, we can't be truly close to God in good times unless we are truly transparent with God in bad times as well. Naomi's story shows us how God reacts when we accuse

God of sending us pain and punishment. Instead of turning away from her in her grief or leaving her to stew in her own bitterness, God continued to offer her grace and love. Even if we turn our backs on God, we can be assured that God will never turn his back on us.

God didn't withhold any future goodness or blessing from Naomi's life just because she was angry with God. Thankfully, there's a lot more to Naomi's story than this first chapter! But she's already taught us an important lesson. It's OK to be honest with God. In fact, God invites us to share our deepest struggles. God wants to be part of both the good and bad parts of our life. When we're feeling discouraged, it's important to remember there are still many chapters to be written in our own stories as well.

When I remember the details of the Christmas now frozen in grief in my mind, I remember not just the shock or the odd details that stuck in my memory. I also remember, looking back, that God was there with us in that moment. The very word *remember* means "to put back together." Our members may be torn from us by grief in a moment, but God walks with us through the difficult moments, hours, and years that follow, helping us put the pieces of our hearts back together so we can breathe again. When we feel lost or forgotten, God remembers us.

Supporting Characters

Although the central figure of the story is Naomi, the book of the Bible that contains her story is named for her daughter-in-law Ruth. In Ruth 1, Naomi gains a gift like no other in the friendship of Ruth. Ruth's name, in fact, means "Friend." These women had been through both joy and grief together, and when Naomi decided to return to her homeland, she urged both of her daughters-in-law to return to their own families. One of them, Orpah, decided to return to her parents, but Ruth refused to go back. Her powerful and beautiful words have become well-known poetry:

> *"Do not press me to leave you*
> *or to turn back from following you!*
> *Where you go, I will go;*
> *where you lodge, I will lodge;*
> *your people shall be my people,*
> *and your God my God.*
> *Where you die, I will die—*
> *there will I be buried.*
> *May the* LORD *do thus and so to me,*
> *and more as well,*
> *if even death parts me from you!"*
> (Ruth 1:16-17)

With these words, Ruth was forming a covenant friendship with Naomi. Their connection as a family was severed by the death of Ruth's husband, Naomi's son. Ruth's covenant reinstated the bonds of family between them. Stronger than a contract, a covenant has at its center the God they would both worship and follow. They would need God's strength to carry them through the difficult days ahead.

As with Naomi and Ruth, God often provides us with strength in a very real and physical way by providing us with each other for support. The spiritual is made real in the tangible, loving support of the people of God in our lives.

Ruth's poetic words bound her in covenant friendship to Naomi, but they also bound her to Naomi's God. They were not just words of camaraderie; they were words of conversion. Where once Naomi and Ruth had shared common love and common grief, now they shared a common faith. While it's important for us to reach out and create friendships with nonbelievers, it's also important for our souls to nurture friendships with others who have faith in Jesus Christ.

Ruth and Naomi faced the common struggle of grief for those they loved and lost. This obstacle strengthened their friendship by giving them a deep understanding for one another's pain. Each of us starts out in life with a family of origin, the family that we are born into and raised in. We end up in life in a family of destination, the family we may marry into, give birth to, or end up living with as adults. There is another kind of family called a family choice. These are people who may have no blood relation to us but may become as close as or closer than family. This kind of friendship can bring us some of the greatest joy and comfort we will ever experience in life.

Ruth made an alliance of friendship with Naomi that went beyond their bloodlines. She chose to reject ties with family members in order to support and protect a friend. Covenant friendship often runs deeper than ties with relatives. One of

God's greatest gifts to us is the gift of friendship. Through our friends, we receive God's love, kindness, laughter, and grace through a human delivery system.

As you reflect on the friendships you've treasured in life, remember the source, the Giver of all good gifts.

A Turning Point

Ruth experienced the same kinds of loss that we see in Naomi's story. She also was grieving the loss of her husband, her father-in-law, and her brother-in-law. She had just left her homeland, including her family and friends and everything familiar and comforting to her, just as Naomi had done after the famine. Ruth must have experienced the same kind of pain and tears that Naomi did. She may have even gone through similar stages of anger and depression. But as we see in Chapter 2, Ruth's grief began to take on a different shape.

When they arrived in Bethlehem, Ruth found herself in a desperate situation. In that particular time and culture, the male members of the household would work to supply food and shelter for their family. Ruth and Naomi had no one to provide for them, a situation that made their grief and loss seem even more hopeless. If no one took action on their behalf, it was possible that they could starve or be forced to beg on the streets.

Instead of wallowing or waiting for someone else to take responsibility, Ruth channeled her grief, worry, and anxiety into action. With Naomi's blessing, she went to the fields each day to glean—to gather the leftovers the harvesters had dropped. She worked tirelessly until sundown, and we're told she worked the entire season until the harvest had finished. Ruth's initiative and determination saved her life and Naomi's, and it set into motion a course of events that would change their lives forever.

When we are feeling stressed and overwhelmed by the circumstances of our own lives, it sometimes helps to look outside ourselves to the needs of others. That seems counterintuitive. If our resources are scarce and our lives frazzled, shouldn't we stay focused on solving our own problems? Isn't it true that "God helps those who help themselves"? Actually, that phrase is nowhere to be found in the Bible. Instead, Scripture offers us a different prescription.

This is a remedy best applied to our own wounds, not to others. When someone is struggling or in pain, it's not helpful to tell them, "It could be worse; go out there and help someone else!" Instead, a listening ear is almost always the best help we can offer. But if we apply this medicine to our own hurts, it often turns out that our example of caring for the needs of others, even when our needs are great, can inspire those who are watching to do the same. That was certainly true in Ruth's case. Her goodness and hard work were noticed and rewarded.

First, Boaz, the owner of the fields in which Ruth worked each day, noticed her determination. He perceived that Ruth was a remarkable young woman. He saw that she wasn't wallowing in self-pity or waiting for someone to take care of her problems for her. And her take-charge attitude inspired Boaz to help her succeed.

When Ruth returned home with an amount of barley that was obviously more than she could have gathered under normal circumstances, Naomi knew something was up. Ruth obviously had had help. Ruth's heart of service toward Naomi inspired Boaz to help her. And in turn, watching Ruth's tireless hard work and kindness and learning of Boaz's acts of compassion helped wake Naomi from her fog of grief. After her bitterness and depression had kept her frozen and immobile for so long, something in Naomi began to melt. Her sense of hope began to return. She saw Ruth's plan of action to keep them alive, and she began to come up with a plan of her own. And that's when things really started to turn around for Ruth and Naomi.

Naomi knew that she and Ruth couldn't live on leftover wheat forever, so she put into action a plan so controversial it had to be done under the cover of darkness. She planned to get Boaz to marry Ruth and restore their family to financial health and standing in the community. And her plan worked! Ruth acted with selflessness, serving Naomi. Boaz acted with integrity, serving and protecting Ruth. Naomi came up with a plan that had daring audacity, one that would reward Ruth for her kindness and ensure a future with hope for all of them.

Peeking ahead to the happy ending of the story, we find that when Boaz and Ruth married and had their first child, they named him Obed, which means "servant." This may seem an unusual name for the son of the boss, the landowner who had servants working for him. Why name their child "servant"? The clue to that mystery can be found by examining the heart of Obed's parents and grandmother. They had servants' hearts, thinking of others before themselves, not unlike the one who would come much later in their family tree.

We worship a God who serves. God came to earth not as a magnificent king but as a lowly rabbi. When the opportunity presented itself for Jesus to sit back and be catered to at his last dinner on earth, he instead took the role of servant, washing the feet of those who followed him. That role of serving those who are dearly loved is one God is still acting on today.

When I start to feel a little underprivileged compared to those who witnessed God's miraculous works firsthand, it helps me to read Naomi's story. When she felt lost and alone in her grief, she didn't see any burning bushes or receive any celestial words of comfort. God didn't part a sea in order for her to travel home, raise her loved ones from the dead, or miraculously multiply anything to feed her and her widowed daughter-in-law. God's works are invisible in Naomi's story, and yet God's presence is certainly felt throughout the book. One of my favorite phrases in Naomi's story is found toward the beginning of Chapter 2. It's actually a turning point in the story, flipping a switch from tragedy to hope:

> *As it happened, she came to the part of the field belonging to Boaz, who was of the family of Elimelech.*
>
> *(Ruth 2:3)*

The phrase "As it happened" could also be translated "As luck would have it." This is one of the greatest understatements in the Bible! The fact that Ruth "coincidentally" ended up in the fields belonging to Boaz, the one person in all of Bethlehem with the position (as a relative of Naomi's husband) and compassion to help Ruth and Naomi, is what brings about the eventual happy ending for all of the members of this family.

"As luck would have it…" "Luck" would have to be smart enough, loving enough, intentional enough, and powerful enough to make sure that of all the fields surrounding Bethlehem, Ruth would find herself in the one place that could turn this story around and drastically change her future—and Naomi's—forever. Luck often gets credit for the things that God is doing behind the scenes.

When we experience something that is inexplicably helpful, timely, or uncanny in the way it specifically meets our needs, we often refer to it as a coincidence. I believe there are fewer true coincidences than we think. As Christians, we need to come to recognize that many of the happy coincidences in life are actually God working behind the scenes for our good. I've heard others refer to them as "God-incidences"—a way of shifting our gratitude from the happenstance forces of fate to the intentional goodness of God.

To Naomi's credit, she recognized right away that God was at work. She was quick to blame God when things went wrong, but now she was quick to praise God when she saw something happening that she knew was too wonderfully planned to be coincidental.

Naomi's realization that God was working for good on her behalf was a turning point for her. She stopped focusing on the negative past and began to work for positive change for a future for her and Ruth. Ruth recognized that if she wanted something to change, she would have to take action. All along God had been acting and working behind the scenes. Those two things together are often a recipe for miracles in our lives. We need both God's powerful action in our lives and our own initiative, joining with God to work for good. Depending on one or the other ignores the fact that God so clearly wants to work in partnership with us in this world. God is at work for our good, and God wants us to join in.

We need both God's powerful action in our lives and our own initiative, joining with God to work for good.

God loves to work in secret and see if we can uncover God's goodness. God is working not only for our good, for each of our small stories, but also for the good of God's creation—for the big story that is always greater than anything we can wrap our minds around. While this is Naomi's story (in a book with Ruth's name on the cover), it is so much bigger than about just Naomi's individual life. What appears to be a happy ending for her is really a beginning of a new and grander story. The grandson whose birth marks the end of her story here, Obed, will grow up to be the grandfather of King David, the most influential king Israel ever knew. Jesus himself, the long-awaited Messiah, eventually would descend from his servant-hearted lineage. Ruth's seemingly accidental choice of fields to glean in is one of many God-incidences that had to happen to make the joyful outcome of this story possible.

The One and Only True Fairy Tale

There is a sense in which Naomi's story, which features her daughter-in-law Ruth, reads almost like a real-life fairy tale. Now that I have a daughter, I feel a certain excitement about a future that includes watching movies about princesses and playing dress up with gowns, pearls, and tiaras. As a girl I loved all the Disney princess movies, the ones that told basically the same story: a princess, beautiful but helpless, finds herself in a dangerous situation and needs someone to rescue her. A prince, of the charming variety, comes along and is enraptured by her loveliness. He fights the battle she needs fought. She is overwhelmed with gratitude, falls into his arms, and they live happily ever after.

But along with nostalgia for the stories I loved as a little girl, I also have a growing wariness about these fairy tales. I'm starting to realize that although those stories captured my imagination and gave me some of my first dreams of romance, they also did me a great disservice. They planted a desire in me for someone to come along when I was in distress, rescue me from my reality, and carry me away to happily-ever-after.

I want to offer my daughter a story big enough to build real dreams on. I want her to dream about a story that will capture her imagination and her longings, but I also want those longings to be ones that will actually be fulfilled. I want her to know that yes, she does need a Savior, and that he is the one who can provide the kind of rescue we *all* need. I don't mind if she wants to dress up as Cinderella or Sleeping Beauty, but I don't want her to learn those stories by heart until I have a chance to tell her another story. A true story. The story of Naomi and Ruth.

In this story, Ruth is the anti-princess (in contrast to the fairy- tale princess). Here's what I love about her:

- She's from the despised land of Moab (and not the chosen people of Israel), but that doesn't stop her from becoming our heroine. Just the fact that an outsider and a refugee gets the starring role means that God doesn't play favorites.

- The central relationship of her story is not a romance but a friendship between women. Our daughters need to know that friendships will be some of the strongest and most meaningful blessings in their lives, and that they should hold tightly to them, even when they think Prince Charming beckons.

- When tragedy strikes and Ruth and Naomi are left without a man to provide for them, Ruth doesn't bemoan the fact that she has no rights, or that she could be left begging on the streets, or worse. Instead of waiting for Prince Charming to do something about her problems, she gets out and finds a solution herself, working in the fields and bringing home the bacon (or in this case, barley) to support herself and Naomi.

- When Naomi plays matchmaker between Ruth and Boaz, the wealthy owner of the field Ruth's been working in, the two women are clearly the ones taking control of their destinies. These are women who aren't afraid to take part in writing their own fairy-tale ending.

Instead of mistaking the romantic relationship of this story for another "Prince Charming" situation, where a man rides in on a white horse to save the helpless women, let's consider the role Boaz plays in the story. When Naomi realizes that Ruth and Boaz have become acquainted, she speaks her first positive words in the whole story after a long line of "Woe is me" negativity. In Hebrew, kinsman-redeemer is *go'el*. That title describes a role given by the law in Leviticus to a man who would help out a family member in distress by "redeeming" them. The law of Israel declared that a kinsman-redeemer was responsible to redeem a relative who had fallen on hard times and needed rescue. This was called the Levirate law.

This last role is why Naomi says Yahweh hasn't forgotten his kindness even to the dead. A true gentleman, a true *go'el*, would marry a widow of his closest male relative and give inheritance to those children even though they'd be considered the children of the deceased. Though that may seem strange to us today, in Naomi's day, the kinsman-redeemer was someone highly valued by family members because they could count on him to come to the rescue when they were desperate. Besides being a human agent with responsibility to help family members, a kinsman-redeemer was also definitely an instrument of God. While the human kinsman-redeemer is working in plain sight, the true redeemer is the one working behind the scenes. Scripture is clear about the fact that God is the ultimate Kinsman-Redeemer. Any human being who takes on that role is simply showing the world how God comes to our rescue when we need help. Scripture uses the word *go'el* to describe God as redeemer.

Ruth and Naomi's story makes it clear that Boaz is not the prince here. He may be the *go'el* redeeming them from a life of poverty and hunger, but God is the great *Go'el* behind the scenes, redeeming their story of grief and brokenness, bringing light where there was only darkness.

The romance in the Book of Ruth is another story with a hidden hero. The true Redeemer peeks from behind the scenes, waiting to see if we can find him whispering an invitation through the story. Transfixed by the happy marriage of Boaz and Ruth, we just might find ourselves caught up in our own love story, one with the Kinsman-Redeemer, who is at work to claim what is lost.

God will not stop until we are found. Each and every one of us needs a rescuer, a redeemer, and we will not find this rescuer in the personal ads. God is always the one behind every earthly rescue and every romance of the truest kind. Just as God was at work in Ruth's story all along, romancing her through every circumstance and saving grace, so God is at work in each of our lives, leading us toward the one and only true happily-ever-after. Move over Snow White. This is the kind of fairy tale we can build dreams on!

Chapter Four

DANIEL

Then Daniel asked the guard whom the palace master had appointed over Daniel, Hananaiah, Mishael and Azariah: "Please test your servants for ten days. Let us be given vegetables to eat and water to drink. You can then compare our appearance with the appearance of the young men who eat the royal rations, and deal with your servants according to what you observe." So he agreed to this proposal and tested them for ten days. At the end of ten days it was observed that they appeared better and fatter than all the young men who had been eating the royal rations. So the guard continued to withdraw their royal rations and the wine they were to drink, and gave them vegetables. To these four young men God gave knowledge and skill in every aspect of literature and wisdom; Daniel also had insight into all visions and dreams.

(Daniel 1:11-17)

Passing on Traditions

When we're little, our parents seem like know-it-alls. They are the ones in control. They seem to hold all the cards, and they always know what they're doing. Imagine my surprise when I became a mom myself to learn that when they hand you your baby for the first time, they don't hand you the secrets that all parents know, the instructions for what to do at every moment, or the answers to all the questions your children will ask.

On the first night home from the hospital with our first baby, I kicked all the relatives out of the house, thinking I had it all under control, imagining our sweet little family of three bonding all alone together. Let's just say that night convinced me of how much I had to learn.

The surprises definitely didn't end in the newborn phase. Lately I'm baffled that I thought parenting one tiny baby was so difficult. Now that he has grown into the little boy trying to run our household and annoy his little sister, taking care of one tiny baby seems like a piece of cake! Someday I will have two teenagers and I'm sure I'll look back and wonder what all the fuss was about when they were little.

Parenting is not for the faint of heart! Running a multi-million-dollar corporation, or a country, is less challenging on some days (not to mention nights) than raising children.

Not only do our children start out in the world physically helpless, dependent on us for their needs of nourishment and safety and shelter; they also are a behavioral and social blank slate. They need to be indoctrinated into the family's culture: the expectations of how family members are to treat one another, behave at the table, speak or wait to be called on, and generally function in this particular group of people. We begin teaching our children about the family's culture from the first day they are born. Even newborns receive messages about how structured or chaotic, loud or quiet, loving or distant the family's culture will be. Families teach some of the same lessons, but each of our families is unique in some ways, with its own values, standards, and habits that make it special. Your own family, for example, may have communicated the importance of getting an education, appreciating music or nature, serving the poor, or respecting the wisdom of elders.

As our children grow, we teach them that our family culture will sometimes differ from those around us: "We don't do that in our family" or "If your friends jumped off a bridge, would you?" Children are absorbing the culture and beliefs of the family around the table at meals, in the car as they are going places, and often just observing our everyday reactions and responses to the world around us.

Passing on Faith

Once upon a time in ancient Jerusalem, four sets of parents began teaching their children what their families believed and what shape their lives were expected to take on the day they were born. They did this by giving them their names. The four boys were named Daniel, Hananiah, Mishael, and Azariah. Their parents knew the first lesson they wanted to teach their sons: that they should honor and worship God in all they did. They felt so strongly about teaching this lesson that they embedded it in their very names. Consider the meanings of their names:

Daniel: God Is My Judge
Hananiah: Yahweh Is gracious
Mishael: Who Is Like God?
Azariah: Yahweh Has Helped

Each time these boys heard their names, they heard a message about a powerful God who loved and cared for them. The suffix "*el*" at the end of Daniel's and Mishael's names can be seen in many of the names of God in Scripture, such as El Shaddai (God Almighty) and El Elyon (Most High God). Other names that include that suffix are Gabriel (strength of God) and Michael (He Who Is Like God).

The unspoken name of God given to Moses at the burning bush was "I AM." Although "I AM" in Hebrew is not pronounceable (YHWH has no vowels), it is sometimes pronounced Jehovah or Yahweh when vowels are added. The name Yahweh forms the suffix -*aniah* or -*iah* at the end of Hananiah and Azariah's names.

We don't know anything else about Daniel, Hananiah, Mishael, and Azariah's families, but we do know that they made a conscious effort from the first day of their lives to teach them about God and let them know that worshiping the one true God was part of the culture they were born into.

I wonder if those families had a sense of the impending destruction of their surrounding culture and way of life. The Babylonians, under the leadership of King Nebuchadnezzar, invaded and destroyed Jerusalem in 605 B.C., destroying the city and the Temple. The four boys with God-centered names were probably in their early teen years when they became prisoners of war, taken to the empire of Babylon when their beloved Jerusalem was destroyed.

Nebuchadnezzar wanted to destroy the culture and convert the people. He wanted to make them Babylonian in culture, education, attitude, and religion. He knew that in order to do that he would need to conquer the hearts and minds of the leaders of the next generation, instilling in them a Babylonian way of life. He did this by taking an entire generation of leaders back to Babylon, where they would be treated not as prisoners of war or as slaves but as trainees for positions of leadership, influence, and power. He knew that if he could convert one generation away from their religion and way of life to his own, he would reach his goal.

Where others saw an opportunity to live a new and lavish lifestyle, Daniel and his friends refused to defile themselves with food and drink that had been offered to Babylonian idols. To eat this food would have meant worshiping those idols. It would have meant a betrayal of their God and all that their parents had instilled in them, starting with their very names.

These young men stood up to the Babylonians, deprived themselves of one incredibly lavish meal after another, and remained true to their names. Their family culture was so embedded in them that even when they were removed from it and transplanted to a pagan environment, their beliefs did not budge. The words of the moms who had been the know-it-alls in their early days still rang in the boys' minds:

If all your friends ate food offered to idols, would you?

Yahweh is gracious (Hananiah)—you can depend on that in the darkest days. *Yahweh has helped* (Azariah) us in the past and will help you through this. These idols are nothing. There is only one true God. Don't worry what others say or think or do. Their opinions don't matter. *Only God is your judge* (Daniel). Follow God's instructions and no others.

That's the kind of strength it takes to hold fast to God's teaching while living in a world where even dinner time is a chance to bow to idols, to give your heart and life to something besides God. We know all too well that Babylon is not the only culture ever to entice its inhabitants to give their hearts and lives to something besides the one true God. Thank God we are not on our own! We have God's spirit within us to guide us, the power and example of Jesus' life, the teachings of those who have led us to him to sustain us, and the stories of the faithful, such as Daniel and his friends, to inspire and encourage us.

Name Change

The four young men in this Bible story were taken from Jerusalem with countless others and transplanted into a strange culture with strange customs and language. The Babylonians wanted to make them feel so at home that they would forget who they were and become completely converted to the language, culture, and religion of Babylon. And one of the first steps toward that end was to change their names.

The Babylonians took the names that these young men's parents had given them to honor God and replaced them with names that honored the idols worshiped in Babylon. Some of the changes even deliberately mocked their original names and the God they had been raised to worship. They became, *Belteshazzar, Shadrach, Meshach,* and *Abednego.* Just to give you an idea of how awful the name change was, Mishael, which means "Who Is Like Yahweh?" became Meshach, "Who Is Like Aku?"

The challenges to their integrity and faithfulness to God were immediate upon arrival in Babylon. Not only were they renamed; their first meal called their beliefs into question. In Babylon they were immediately confronted with the choice of whether to eat food sacrificed to idols, a form of idol worship. We may think, *What's the big deal? It's just a plate of food!* Temptation often starts small. Think of Eve and Adam and a single piece of fruit. No big deal, right? The small temptations toward a white lie, a selfish action, a glance at a website, an unseen act are the most difficult because no one will know but God and us. These young men were able to withstand the temptation to gorge themselves on delicious food because they knew it would betray the God they loved.

If eating food that had been on the altar of idols seemed like a small thing, Hananiah, Mishael, and Azariah were given bigger challenges soon enough. They faced a decision about whether to bow down to the ninety-foot-high golden idol statue built by King Nebuchadnezzar. They must have stood out, quite literally, as the crowd around them bowed, and they were the sole people left standing in the presence of the huge idol. Standing for God when the rest of the world bows down to things that do not honor God forces us to call on God for help, to remember who God has called us to be, and to remind ourselves that who we are is not supposed to match up with the crowd around us.

It's OK to stand out. In fact, God's people are to be obviously different from everyone else. God created laws for God's people that would make it obvious to the world around them that they were different. God expected them to act in ways that were clearly out of sync with the world around them. This was no accident; it was a strategy to make the world take notice. God's people are different because God is different from anything and anyone else.

When Hananiah, Mishael, and Azariah made the right decision to stand up to a law that ordered them to worship idols, they weren't rewarded; they were punished. The king's anger burned so greatly that he ordered them to be tied and thrown into a blazing furnace heated seven times hotter than usual, mirroring the combustion of his rage. It's important for us to remember that just because we follow God's will does not mean we're immune to the earthly consequences of our actions, however unfair they may be. Hananiah, Mishael, and Azariah weren't excused from the fiery furnace just because they did the right thing in God's eyes. The miracle came, though, when those watching saw not three people in the fire, but four! We're told that the fourth was "like the Son of God" (Daniel 3:25 KJV).

We can't always be sure of our earthly safety because we are God's followers, but we can be sure that God goes with us into the most fiery of situations. When we stand for God, we don't stand alone; God always stands with us.

We can't always be sure of our earthly safety because we are God's followers, but we can be sure that God goes with us into the most fiery of situations.

Back to Daniel

When Daniel worshiped, it took him beyond the borders of Babylon and back to the Temple in Jerusalem where he had worshiped as a boy. As he worshiped and prayed to God, Daniel was no longer a prisoner in a foreign land; he was a citizen of the kingdom of God. So, when a decree from King Darius said that no one could worship or pray to anyone but the king for a full month, Daniel was put in a tough situation.

His three friends had faced a law that attempted to force them to worship something false. Now he was faced with a law that tried to force him *not* to worship something true. This law was orchestrated by his enemies, who were deliberately trying to trap him.

Daniel prayed three times every day in the same place, facing the direction of Jerusalem. Everyone knew about his prayer routine; and it tells us a lot about him. We know that he was faithful to worship God even in this foreign land where he was surrounded by a false religion. How easy it would have been to believe God was far away, unfeeling, or uncaring. Yet Daniel turned to God in prayer faithfully.

Worship gives deep gladness to the heart of God. It also grounds us in a reality that is unseen— one that is truer than those before our eyes.

When we are struggling with harsh realities or simply the monotony of daily life, praising God is often not at the top of our list of things we feel like doing. But our need to worship God does not change with our shifting circumstances. Daniel made worship a habit. If we will do the same, we will find that praise grounds us in a reality beyond our moods or our situations. Worship gives deep gladness to the heart of God. It also grounds us in a reality that is unseen—one that is truer than those before our eyes.

Daniel found a place to worship even when it wasn't convenient or safe. He prayed to God when he may have felt very distant from God. This daily practice of prayer and worship helped Daniel and his friends keep their faith strong when faced with tough choices. Daniel's prayer life and his ability to stay true to God, continuing to worship even when it meant his life was at stake, are intrinsically connected. His continual seeking of God's heart through worship helped him do what was right even when the stakes were high—even when it meant being thrown into a lions' den.

Don't miss that: Worship prepared Daniel to face the lions' den!

From the very beginning, God knew that worship would be as important to us as the air we breathe. When we're living in an atmosphere that could choke the faith out of us, making worship a priority is as important as taking oxygen on a deep-sea diving expedition. The emphasis on worship is found throughout Scripture. The Psalms are packed with praise and worship to God. Revelation shines with technicolor images of worship before the Lamb on the throne. The Book of Exodus dedicates thirteen chapters to instructions about the building of the Tabernacle, a traveling center of worship for God's people. The attention given to worship in so many situations in the Bible shows us how important worship is to God.

Solitary prayer, like Daniel practiced from the window that faced Jerusalem in his room each day, is an important part of the Christian life. As important as it is to pray alone, it is also vital to our spiritual health to gather and worship together.

Getting together with brothers and sisters of faith makes our individual voices of praise, confession, and petition one strong common voice lifted to God. Worshiping together helps keep us from wandering off on our own diversions, bonds us with other believers, and reminds us that we are never alone.

Daniel, Hananiah, Mishael, and Azariah had the benefit of being together in exile. While they didn't have their families or their homeland, they had each other, a fact that likely helped sustain them and guide them in the tough choices they were forced to make.

There are stories from many other wars in history that show how faith and solidarity sustained men and women like Daniel and his friends after they had been captured by the enemy—stories of prisoners of war passing Bibles back and forth and whispering verses and hymns through cell walls (acts of worship). These acts, though small, gave them hope. Although we aren't imprisoned, we do live in a land that is not our home. Knowing that we are not alone in our faith has an amazing effect of helping us stay spiritually alive in the most difficult of times. Worship is the redirection of our hearts to the heart of God. It's the corporate gathering of God's people into one family. It's the pure oxygen we need to breathe to keep our faith alive!

The Problem with Idols

We human beings are innately created to worship. It's part of our makeup as spiritual beings. We all assign the role of God to something. To find out what that might be, we only have to follow the paper trail left in our bank statements, calendars, and journals. If we track the decisions and motivations recorded in those three records, we'll discover what we truly value. Worship is more than just belief. It means orienting our lives to give honor to something beyond ourselves. Whatever we put at the center of our lives is what we worship.

Worshiping an invisible God takes quite a leap of faith. It's so much easier to believe in what we can see and touch with our hands than in a God we cannot see. To fix this problem, the Babylonians (and many other cultures like them) made idols, physical statues or representations of their gods. These were made of wood or metal and placed on an altar where people could worship them, bow to them, and make sacrifices to them.

As we've seen, the leaders of Babylon tried to force Daniel, Hananiah, Mishael, and Azariah to take God from the center of their lives and worship false gods and idols instead. Since God held a place of honor in their names, the Babylonian leaders took away those names and replaced them with names honoring false gods; and the gods at the center of their new names were Bel, Aku, and Nebo.

Daniel became Belteshazzar. *Bel* signifies the title "Lord" or "Master" rather than a proper name. This title was possibly used to signify Marduk, one of many Babylonian gods. Hananiah and Mishael became Shadrach and Meshach, with the idol Aku at the heart of their new names, the Babylonian god of wisdom. Azariah became Abednego, to honor Nebo, the Babylonian god of the moon.

The Bible addresses the damaging nature of idol worship in a poetic chapter of Isaiah, where the prophet actually brings up some of the exact idols mentioned in the new names Daniel and his friends received:

> *Bel bows down, Nebo stoops low;*
> > *their idols are borne by beasts of burden.*
> *The images that are carried about are burdensome,*
> > *a burden for the weary.*
> *They stoop and bow down together;*
> > *unable to rescue the burden,*
> > *they themselves go off into captivity.*
> > > *(Isaiah 46:1-2 NIV)*

The imagery of these first two verses is of large, heavy idols placed on the backs of donkeys or oxen to be moved. Instead of powerfully lifting burdens, the idols themselves become a burden. Instead of freeing people from captivity, they themselves can be carried into captivity.

God's objection to people worshiping false idols is less about God's need for adoration and more about how horribly it affects our lives when we give our worship away to the wrong things. God insists that we worship God alone, rather than idols, not because God is self-interested but because abiding in God's character is in our best interest.

God wants us to orient our lives to worship the only thing that can unburden us: God! That's how much God loves us. He mourns the fact that while people should be bowing to the God who made them and can save them, instead they are carrying around heavy idols. In the images of Isaiah 46, God ridicules the idols for themselves bowing down because they are causing such a burden to the people and animals forced to carry them.

Instead of lifting people's burdens, these idols cause an extra burden on their lives, adding to the burdens they were hoping the idols would help alleviate. The truth is that idol worship damages our lives. It's a tragic irony that the very idols we suppose will save us are the things that destroy us.

God loves us so fiercely that he fights to destroy anything that could harm us. It's no accident that when God hands out the Ten Commandments for the people to follow that they begin with these two:

> *I am the* LORD *your God, who brought you*
> *out of the land of Egypt, out of the house*
> *of slavery; you shall have no other gods*
> *before me.*
>
> *You shall not make for yourself an idol,*
> *whether in the form of anything that is in*
> *heaven above, or that is on the earth beneath,*
> *or that is in the water under the earth. You*
> *shall not bow down to them or worship them;*
> *for I the* LORD *your God am a jealous God,*
> *punishing children for the iniquity of parents,*
> *to the third and fourth generation of those*
> *who reject me, but showing steadfast love to a*

> *thousandth generation of those who love me*
> *and keep my commandments.*
>
> *(Exodus 20:2-6)*

Only God can save. God brought the Israelites out of Egypt, where they were slaves. This reminder is closely connected to the command that they should have no other gods and should not make idols. The implication is that when we turn to anything but God for help, we are deceiving ourselves, burdening ourselves, and separating ourselves from the help and salvation God is so eager to give. The benefits of choosing to worship God impact not only our own lives but also trickle down to thousands of generations that will follow.

While our current culture doesn't often create physical idols to represent false gods (statues of clay and wood and bronze), we do have a problem with idol worship. We adopt things in our own lives and place them in the seat that God alone should occupy. We may take relationships or control, worry or financial resources, jobs or children, desires for food or sex, beauty or wealth, and begin to make them the center of our thoughts and priorities. The question at the heart of the Book of Daniel is this: *What will you worship?*

Daniel and his three friends are given that choice again and again. Will you eat food offered to idols? Will you bow down to a golden statue? Will you pray to the king instead of praying daily to the God you love? Each conflict they face, each major choice they make, is about choosing whom they will worship.

**The most basic conflicts of our lives arise when we
begin to worship things besides God.**

The same is true for us. The most basic conflicts of our lives arise when we begin to worship things besides God. When we turn our lives over to God, our most basic records (like our checkbook, calendar, and journal) will indicate choices that honor God, decisions we've made because we want to be more like God. God's name and character will shine through the line items, daily entries, and appointments, and our lives will reflect God's joy because of it. Idols will always burden us. God will always lift our burdens.

All-Out Worship

An awareness of the ways our hearts easily slip into the worship of other things is the first step in turning them back to God. When we remind ourselves again that God is the source of our comfort and strength, the giver of every good and perfect gift, the choice to worship God with our whole lives flows naturally. I hope that you have discovered the joy of worshiping the One who unburdens, who lifts up, who brings peace and contentment. In a world filled with competitors for our attention, God is the one choice as object of our affection who will give more love than he could ever receive.

The account of Hananiah, Mishael, and Azariah in the fiery furnace found in Daniel 3 ends with them walking out of the furnace without a mark on them, unsinged and unharmed. King Nebuchadnezzar, who had ordered them burned to death, was impressed, to say the least, but he wasn't impressed with them; he clearly saw that their actions pointed beyond them to the God they represented.

A similar change occurred in the heart of a king when Daniel defied King Darius's decree that no one could pray to any god or man except him and he was sentenced to be thrown into a den of lions. When Daniel survived a night in the lions' den, King Darius changed his tune completely. Instead of demanding that all people pray only to the king, he issued another decree—that his people pray to the God of Daniel.

God calls us to live so differently from the people around us that they take notice. He calls us to live the way Jesus did. Daniel, Hananiah, Mishael, and Azariah had God's name embedded in their own names. When we make a pledge to follow Jesus, he gives us the name "Christian" to wear—a title that has the very name of Christ embedded in it. If we allow him to continually transform our hearts and actions, we will bring honor and praise not to ourselves but to Christ.

For each of these men of God, the story could have looked much different. They could have turned their backs on God in fear for their lives. They could have hidden away, pretending to worship the king but praying to God in secret. They could have felt abandoned by God and given up the idea of God's faithfulness. But they didn't! They stuck close to God, they remembered who they were, and they let God write an incredible story—one that almost seems like the stuff of fairy tales. Walking out of a furnace unscathed and out of a lions' den without a scratch are the kinds of storylines that God wants to write in our lives. When we trust and obey like Daniel and his friends, we'll see God write amazing stories in us!

Chapter Five

PETER

Now when Jesus came into the district of Caesarea Philippi, he asked his disciples, "Who do people say that the Son of Man is?" And they said, "Some say John the Baptist, but others Elijah, and still others Jeremiah or one of the prophets." He said to them, "But who do you say that I am?" Simon Peter answered, "You are the Messiah, the Son of the living God." And Jesus answered him, "Blessed are you, Simon son of Jonah! For flesh and blood has not revealed this to you, but my Father in heaven. And I tell you, you are Peter, and on this rock I will build my church, and the gates of Hades will not prevail against it."

(Matthew 16:13-18)

God Chooses Fixer-Uppers

When I answered the call to follow Jesus, I was a mess—selfish and immature. As it became clear to me that God loved me and wanted better than a first-draft life for me, I often had doubts that I was worthy of God's love. I wasn't sure why God would choose me to be a follower, much less a leader.

I remember thinking that the people in the Bible were perfect, holy examples for us to follow—examples I knew I'd never live up to. After all, why did we call them "Saint Matthew" or "Saint John" on our church signs? When I got to the story of Simon, however, there was no denying that this guy was no saint! I remember reading about Simon Peter's antics, trying hard to figure out why this perfectly flawed person had been given such a central place in Jesus' perfect story. It helped me figure out that while he wasn't a saint, he was an ordinary man that I could identify with. If God loved Simon Peter and thought God could use him for good, there might just be hope for me as well!

When Simon answered the call to follow Jesus, he was a mess. He was impulsive, brash, immature, and reckless. His temper flared and he usually spoke up before his brain could intervene. Jesus knew he had his work cut out for him where Simon was concerned. But for some reason, Jesus chose Simon. Not only was he chosen to be a follower; he was chosen as a leader for the disciples and the ragtag collection of imperfect people who would come to be called the church.

How do we know that Jesus singled out Simon Peter as a leader? Four times in the New Testament the disciples are listed, as if in a roll call, in the books of Matthew, Mark, Luke, and Acts. The order in which they are named varies slightly. But each time they are listed in an order that basically can be divided into three groups of four. In all four passages, the groups of four remain the same, and the groups are always given in the same order. Although the order in which the disciples are named changes slightly within some of the groups of four, the placements within the first and last groups give us clues about the disciple who received the most honor and the one who was least on the list.

The biblical authors couldn't resist listing Judas last every time. In the lists from three of the Gospels, they give away the end of the story by telling us from the very moment the disciples are chosen that Judas will betray Jesus. Acts doesn't name him at all since his story had already come to an end.

The first group of disciples is the list of the four who were closest to Jesus— two sets of brothers who were the first disciples Jesus called. And always at the top of that list, always named first in the first group, is Simon Peter. His position at the top of the list marks him as the leader and spokesperson of the disciples. The rough, impetuous fisherman is an unlikely but clear selection to lead the disciples and the future church.

Simon leads the group in many of the Gospel stories. Sometimes his leadership is intentional, planned, and strategic. Sometimes it seems almost accidental—an inadvertent by-product of his reckless, impulsive nature. Sometimes the other disciples seem to hang back, letting Simon stick his neck out and take the risks they don't want to take.

Although his risky behavior sometimes gets him in trouble, there are times when he lands on the right answer, almost by accident. Never was that more true than on the day that Jesus changed Simon's name and began to rewrite his story. Jesus was giving his disciples a pop quiz. He first asked them, "Who do others say that I am?" It was easy to tell Jesus what they had overheard from the crowds of people around them.

Once they had passed the easy portion of the test, Jesus asked them: "Who do *you* say that I am?" It was one of those questions that required them to think about all they had heard and seen in their time with Jesus, to put the facts together, and then to create an answer that matched their experiences, observations, beliefs, and feelings about Jesus. They all hesitated at that point. All of them, that is, except Simon.

I doubt that Simon stopped to think about what the other disciples would think of him, or if he had the right answer or an answer that Jesus would like. In keeping with his impulsive nature, he probably went with his gut and simply reacted.

No one had told Simon that Jesus was the Messiah (the Christ), the one that all of Israel had awaited for so long. He seemed to blurt it out in a moment of passion. And for once it was just the right thing to say: "Simon Peter answered, 'You are the Messiah, the Son of the living God'" (Matthew 16:16).

Jesus isn't just interested in what we've overheard about him from others. He wants to know what we believe about him ourselves. You can tell Jesus what your parents say about him, what your pastors and church leaders say about him, what you've read about him in books or overheard about him from friends or acquaintances, and he'll still keep asking, "But who do you say that I am?"

Simon was transparent, honest, and personal in his response. Instead of speaking from a carefully measured academic lecture or religious sermon, he spoke from his heart. And he acknowledged that Jesus was the one he personally had been waiting for, the one who was changing his life and could change the world. Jesus rewarded Simon with a response that must have stunned the other disciples: "Blessed are you, Simon son of Jonah! For flesh and blood has not revealed this to you, but my Father in heaven. And I tell you, you are Peter, and on this rock I will build my church, and the gates of Hades will not prevail against it" (Matthew 16:17-18).

The name *Simon* means "He hears and obeys." This name had hung around his neck like an oversized sweater that never quite fit. He never really listened much. He was too busy blurting out the first thing on his mind. And obedience? That continued to be a struggle for him throughout the Gospel stories.

The name *Peter* means "rock, boulder." It describes a solid foundation. At first it doesn't seem any more appropriate than the name he had before. But what Jesus says next tells us something about his reasoning for choosing this impetuous follower to lead the pack.

The phrase "I will build" means that Jesus was willing to call someone who was a work in progress, someone on whom he could build a vision, a foundation for the future of his church. Jesus was claiming Simon because he was great building material, not because he was a finished product.

The reasons Jesus is attracted to us as followers—the magnetic pull to do everything in his power to make us one of his own—has nothing to do with anything we've already built ourselves up to be. It has everything to do with his unconditional love for us just as we are.

The most muddled personality in Jesus' hands is worth more in the kingdom of God than the person who seems to have it all together but denies God access and authority in her or his life. Peter is living proof of that! Aren't you glad God calls us just the way we are? If God waited for us to become perfect in order to qualify us as followers, God would be waiting forever. We simply don't have the ability to make ourselves good enough for God; so God comes to us where we are and scoops us up as if we were a rare and precious asset, while those around us shake their heads wondering what God sees in us. Amid the world's choruses of "That one will never be a saint!" God enjoys proving them wrong.

Peter's Up-and-Down Storyline

Peter's story reads like a journal of life's ups and downs. If we could read the stories about him in the Gospels from *his* point of view, we would likely hear about his excitement and apprehension upon leaving his whole life behind to follow

Jesus. We would learn how his world was shaken when Jesus changed his name to "Rock" and declared that he would use him as a foundation on which to build the church. But right alongside his exhilaration and accomplishment, we'd also hear of his setbacks, the way his flaws tended to rear their ugly heads again and again.

If we could read Peter's own journals through the years, we would see that some of the same struggles he had before meeting Jesus popped up again in the years that followed. Like most of us, his old life seemed to follow him like a shadow. He possessed both a desire to change and a resistance to change that makes his life resemble a spiritual yo-yo. While Peter did change and grow as he walked with Jesus, the same flaws he had as a brash fisherman when Jesus called him beside the sea were still present even after he became the leader of the disciples.

Just as quickly as Peter became the hero of the day through his understanding of Jesus' identity as Messiah, his *misunderstanding* of the role of Messiah instantly made him a hindrance to God's mission. In that moment the *Rock* that was meant to be a foundation for Jesus' message became a stumbling block. Peter learned in that moment that his words not only could make him a mouthpiece for God; they also could make him a tool of the evil one, a stumbling block standing in the way of the very calling that Jesus had come to earth to fulfill.

That had to be a low blow, going from your Savior calling you rock to referring to you as Satan (Matthew 16:23). The noun and proper name *Satan* is actually derived from a Hebrew verb meaning "to obstruct" or "to oppose." When Peter thought he was doing Jesus a favor by telling him he would never suffer and die in such a horrible manner, he was actually obstructing Jesus' path, putting himself in the way of Jesus' ultimate purpose on earth. And that's only the first time in Scripture that we see Peter reverting back to his old ways.

At the Last Supper, in a shocking act of servanthood, Jesus offered to wash the disciples' feet. Instead of celebrating the moment or waiting to see what Jesus might be trying to teach him, Peter recoiled and rebuked Jesus: "'No!' [he] said. 'You will never wash my feet!'" (John 13:8 CEB). After Jesus explained his purpose in washing their feet, Peter begged for Jesus to wash all of him (John 13:9). Again Peter's impulsivity brought to light both the worst and the best in his heart.

When it comes to transformation in our lives, most of us would love a microwave solution, one where we could watch change unfolding quickly through a little window.... More often, though, God works with us in the slow movement of grace that takes a lifetime.

The Bible often uses Peter's old and new names interchangeably, even after Jesus elevated him to rocklike status with his name change. The truth is that sometimes Peter lived up to his new name. Other times he acted more like his pre-Jesus self. At those times Jesus called him Simon, pointing out that he was acting like his old self and not the rock that Jesus had called him to become.

Simon Peter is a hybrid of his two names, which also appears in Scripture, reminding us (and him) that transformation doesn't happen overnight—that often we are living with both our old nature and our new hope, all in one self.

When it comes to transformation in our lives, most of us would love a microwave solution, one where we could watch change unfolding quickly through a little window. Sometimes that happens. I've known people who have experienced freedom from a lifelong temptation or have been transformed in just one moment. More often, though, God works with us in the slow movement of grace that takes a lifetime.

Sometimes we have the idea that a life committed to Christ will be instantly better. This gives people the expectation that the moment their lives are in Jesus' hands, they won't struggle anymore—that their flaws will melt away and their temptations will fade. That way of thinking is similar to the idea that many people have about marriage—that saying "I do" will automatically transform the couple into new persons. We say it all the time: "You just need to find someone and settle down," as if getting married will automatically settle you down—make you more stable, more dependable, more mature. A lot of people find out the hard way that the only thing getting married makes you is married. You have to work at the growing up part together.

Likewise, the only thing giving your life to Christ makes you is a Christian. All the same temptations, all the same struggles, all the same character flaws that drove you into the arms of Christ will follow you there. The difference is that Jesus is there to help you with all of it. Jesus is the one with the power to enable each of us to live a transformed life.

Sanctification, the process of change that makes us more and more like Jesus, is more like a slow cooker than a microwave. Even as we walk with God, we sometimes will fall down again, often in the same potholes we fell into before. But there is always hope and grace and forgiveness. I'm grateful that God has the patience and grace to work on us over the long haul, when we would have given up on ourselves long ago. The change is there, though it may be barely perceptible at times. We'd like to see a lightning-fast transformation, but we need to remember that the process of change we are going through is as important as the end result itself.

Peter's journey is characterized by ups and downs along the way. Sometimes he shows his rocklike faith by walking on water to meet Jesus. Sometimes he sinks like a stone. But he changes and grows and ultimately lives into the name Jesus has given him.

Your journey likely has ups and downs as well. Sometimes you may look like a poster child for the changes faith can bring. Other times you may find yourself sinking back into your old habits. Up or down, know that God is with you, and that God's love for you does not change with the whims of your behavior. God is writing a new story for your life, and that story has grace spelled out on every page.

God's Arithmetic

No one needed God's grace more than Peter. We've already seen Peter's pattern of ups and downs throughout his walk with Jesus. Now let's look at how Jesus responded to the low points in Peter's story.

As with each of the Gospels, the order in which events are shared in the Gospel of Matthew has specific meaning. As we've seen, Peter's high point when he acknowledged Jesus as the Son of God (Matthew 16:17-18) was quickly followed by his low point when he said Jesus must not suffer and die (Matthew 16:23). What would we expect to happen next? For Peter to be kicked out of the group? Demoted from the position of leader?

It's clear that Jesus didn't give up on Peter; instead, he continued to invite Peter into his inner circle, even bringing Peter with him in the select group of disciples who had the amazing privilege of witnessing what we have come to call the Transfiguration, a moment of Jesus' heavenly glory on earth (Matthew 17). Through the highs and the lows, Jesus continued his work of transformation in Peter's life.

One time, Jesus admonished Peter by using his old name not once but twice. The disciples were gathered in the upper room for the Last Supper. After supper, an argument arose about who would be the greatest in the kingdom of heaven.

It was then that this exchange took place between Jesus and Peter:

> *"Simon, Simon, listen! Satan has demanded to*
> *sift all of you like wheat, but I have prayed for*
> *you that your own faith may not fail; and you,*
> *when once you have turned back, strengthen*
> *your brothers." And he said to him, "Lord,*
> *I am ready to go with you to prison and to*
> *death!" Jesus said, "I tell you, Peter, the cock*
> *will not crow this day, until you have denied*
> *three times that you know me."*
> (Luke 22:31-34)

Peter blurted out that he would never be the one to betray Jesus, to disappoint the Savior he loved. Jesus knew better. He predicted that before the rooster crowed, Peter would deny Jesus not once but three times. And that's exactly what happened.

Jesus knew that Peter would disappoint him by denying him. But he also knew that Peter wouldn't stay down long. He prayed that this moment of struggle would be one that would strengthen Peter, and that when he bounced back he would strengthen his brothers as well.

There are numerous examples of these up-and-down moments in Scripture when Peter is referred to by his old name as well as his new name. But even more often in Scripture he is referred to as Simon Peter, a nod to his old and new nature mixed together in one. If we're honest, most of us are also a mix of the old and the new, a work in progress with Jesus gradually helping us subtract the negative and add the positive. If we learn anything from Peter, it's that it certainly takes some time to work out our spiritual kinks.

It's no accident that the number three appears over and over again in Peter's story, helping tie the pieces together. Even though his story is recorded in fragments by the authors of all four Gospels, each of them remembered to mention the number that became very significant in Peter's story.

After Jesus asked the *three* leading disciples to stay awake and pray with him, he returned *three* times to find them sleeping. When Jesus was arrested and dragged away to be beaten and put on trial, Peter followed at a distance. Those events must have seemed so unbelievable, so horrible. In the middle of it all, *three* different people recognized Peter as a follower of Jesus. At the very moment Jesus needed Peter's support the most, strong Peter melted into the old Simon and denied that he even knew Jesus—not once, not twice, but *three* times. His mind must have flashed back to the conversation when Jesus predicted that betrayal. The feelings of failure and shame must have been overwhelming to Peter. Not only had he let down his Savior; he had done it even after Jesus had predicted it and warned him!

This is when Peter needed forgiveness the most. This was his moment of greatest need, and this is where Jesus really triumphed. It's at our times of greatest need that Jesus can show us the greatest forgiveness, and forgiveness was what those few days were all about. Within hours of Peter's denial,

Jesus was hanging on a cross, taking on the sins of the world. Even more important to Peter must have been the realization that Jesus was taking on *his* sins as well.

Somehow when God is balancing the equation of grace, one innocent figure on a cross can equal forgiveness for all of humanity.

Here is where the arithmetic of God just doesn't add up to the rest of the world. Somehow when God is balancing the equation of grace, one innocent figure on a cross can equal forgiveness for all of humanity. One of the ironies of God's arithmetic on the cross is that Peter already had had one math lesson in forgiveness. He was the one who sometime before had asked Jesus to set limits on forgiveness.

In Matthew 18:21-22, Peter asked Jesus how often he should forgive. Some translations describe the number that Jesus gave as "seventy-seven times." In others it's translated "seventy times seven." Think about it. To keep count of someone's sins against you all the way up to 490 would require some serious, grudge-bearing sin accounting! Jesus is expressing that the number of times we forgive should be more than we can even keep count of.

Of all the times Simon Peter should have been grateful for a math lesson, it was that one, because it turned out he was going to need it. "How many times should we forgive someone,

Lord? Five, six, seven? Should I keep count on my fingers?" After denying Jesus, Peter was definitely in need of a *seventy-times-seven* kind of forgiveness. And the days surrounding Jesus' crucifixion and resurrection were a perfect time to see Jesus put that promise into action.

When Jesus and Peter finally met up again, things were different. Jesus, for one, had paid the price for the sins of all of humanity, risen from the dead, and conquered the grave. He had been a little busy. Peter, on the other hand, had decided to go fishing.

The symmetry of this story in John is a beautiful thing— the way that Jesus met Peter in the exact place where they had begun; the way that he gave a fishing lesson to the most seasoned fishermen and the nets were so full they almost broke. Speaking of math—this storyteller cares so much about detail that he even lets us know exactly how many fish were caught that day (John 21:11).

When Jesus called out to Peter, "Follow me," it must have felt like déjà vu. Those were the words of his original calling. Now they were the words that called him back, letting him know that Jesus wanted him to follow in the same way as he did that first day, just as much now that Jesus had seen him at his worst as in the very beginning.

"Simon, do you love me?" Jesus asked. After giving three knife-in-the-heart denials the night before Jesus died, Peter received three chances to answer this all-important question. With each question, Jesus used his old name, Simon. Using this name said, "I know who you are, and I love you anyway.

I know your struggle and pain, and I know that you are your own worst enemy; and I'm still here to offer you help."

Three times Peter fell asleep in the garden. "Simon, are you asleep? Could you not keep awake one hour?" (Mark 14:37).

Three times Peter denied Jesus as predicted. "Simon, Simon, Satan has asked to sift...you like wheat" (Luke 22:31 NLT).

Three times Jesus gave Peter a chance to reform, repent, and answer the most personal question possible, each time using the most personal, first-name address:

> *"Simon son of John, do you love me more than these?"...*
>
> *"Simon son of John, do you love me?"...*
>
> *"Simon son of John, do you love me?"...*
> (John 21:15-17)

Suddenly it all added up. It didn't matter to Jesus who the world said that he was; he had wanted to know, "Who do you say that I am?" It didn't matter to him what Simon had done. He wanted to know, "Do you love me?" And three times Simon jumped at the chance to answer "Yes!"

Jesus' questions are personal. He wants our answers to be equally personal. It doesn't matter to him what we have done. What matters to him is what we believe about him and how we answer the question "Do you love me?"

I often stumble, showing my old colors beneath all the work Jesus has done in me. I tell Jesus "Never!" when I should say, "Anything you ask, Lord." I fall asleep when I should be standing by him. I betray and deny him not once but over and over. And yet Jesus still finds the sum of my behavior to be nothing compared to his great love and sacrifice for me.

For every mistake you make, Jesus adds one more chance. He doesn't subtract his grace or mercy. He doesn't take away the chance of a fresh start. He continually goes before you and asks you to follow him. If you betray him seven times, he gives you eight chances to redeem yourself. If you mess up seventy-times-seven times, God's arithmetic responds with seventy-times-seven-plus-one offers of forgiveness, followed by an invitation just like the first: "Follow me."

Jesus always offers us another chance to answer that singularly most important question: "Do you love me?"

Yes, Lord. A thousand times, yes!

Chapter Six

AN UNNAMED WOMAN

Early in the morning he came again to the temple. All the people came to him and he sat down and began to teach them. The scribes and the Pharisees brought a woman who had been caught in adultery; and making her stand before all of them, they said to him, "Teacher, this woman was caught in the very act of committing adultery. Now in the law Moses commanded us to stone such women. Now what do you say?" They said this to test him, so that they might have some charge to bring against him.

(John 8:2-6a)

Introductions

Learning someone's name is usually the first step in getting to know that person. You probably wouldn't ask about the person's occupation or family until you at least knew his or her name. You certainly wouldn't think of asking about his or her deepest hurts, wildest dreams, or closest moment to God if you had never even been properly introduced.

Somehow the Bible didn't get the memo about the etiquette of introductions. Scripture is full of some of the most famously anonymous people that ever lived. It feels awkward sometimes to read the stories of the intimate details of people's lives and never learn their identity. We often know their heart's desire, the depth of their pain, and the way that Jesus changed their destiny without even being able to call them by name.

We call them things such as the blind beggar, the man lowered through the roof by his friends, the woman at the well, the rich young ruler, the woman who washed Jesus' feet, the boy with the five loaves and two fish, Potiphar's wife, Lot's wife, Noah's wife, and Job's wife. They were important enough to make it into the Bible, but somehow no one thought to catch their names. We've assigned each one a nickname based on his or her circumstances, actions, or relationships, whether good or bad.

The woman we'll look at in this chapter is one whose nickname—often written in Scripture in bold as a title above the first paragraph of her story—is a devastating label. Because of a mistake, a moment in her life she must not have been particularly proud of, she received a nickname that marks her in every Bible that has ever been printed. She is known only as "The Woman Caught in Adultery."

I don't know about you, but if you rewound the story of my life and picked out my worst moments, I wouldn't want to be known by them for posterity. I would hate it even more if I were to be known for the rest of history by the names that I was called or that I internally called myself during my toughest times.

This woman was dragged onstage in the opening act of her own story by a group of men who were, shall we say, a little too excited about someone else's sin. They were probably keyed up and out of breath, calling out to Jesus in animated voices: "Jesus! Here's a woman caught in the very moment of her sin! We know what the Law says should be done with a woman like this. Since you're teaching on the Law, since you think you're qualified to say what is right and wrong here, what do you say? Judge her case for us."

It's clear from the story that these men weren't interested in justice. They weren't even interested in the woman. What they are interested in is Jesus—specifically, catching him in a trap, a theological Catch-22.

If Jesus agreed with them and with the law of Moses, saying they should stone her, he would be seizing power away from the law of Rome, and the Romans would have his head. If he said she should go free without punishment, he would be defying the law of Moses and likely would lose the respect of the crowds who had been following him.

They had Jesus cornered right where they wanted him. At the least, they could split the crowd's opinion of him, reducing the size of his following by half. And if they were successful, they might even set in motion events that would lead not to the woman's execution but to Jesus' own death.

If they truly had been interested in sin and law and justice, there likely would have been another person present and named in the story. Let me give you a hint. It takes two to tango! Where is the man caught in adultery? There is no being caught in the act of adultery by yourself; so somehow in their careful plot they've caught only half of the perpetrators, letting the other go free.

According to Jewish law, no one could be proven guilty without the testimony of two witnesses. You couldn't just be "the woman accused of adultery" or "the woman suspected of adultery." You had to be caught in the act, and you had to be caught by two eyewitnesses. So these men must have gone to a lot of trouble to have two people catch this woman in the act while, at the same time, letting her partner slip out the back door.

The way they used her for their own agenda, shaming her in a public place (the Temple, no less) shows just how little concern they had for her as a person. It's possible that she had been treated with contempt by other men in her life, that she was all too familiar with men who used her for their own purposes without truly knowing her heart, her hurts, or even her name.

Now standing before her was one more man. Even if she didn't know much about Jesus, it was clear immediately that he was teaching in the Temple as a rabbi, a teacher of the very law that she was accused of breaking. One condemning word from him and she'd be dragged out and stoned. A forgiving word and her life would be spared. She must have wondered what this man would do with her. Her life was in his hands.

As onlookers to her story, we have the benefit of information that our frightened, unnamed friend did not have in those anxious moments. We know the good news that the man standing before her was different than anyone she had ever met. He wasn't only a man; he was also her Creator and her God, and he loved her more than anyone ever could.

As the old country song goes, she had been "looking for love in all the wrong places"; but finally she was standing in the right place. Finally, she was standing face-to-face with the source of true love. This was the one place she would find fulfillment of the deep need for love that she had sought to fill in the arms of another man who could never love her enough. And her life would never be the same.

Her story is definitely one of the most powerful anonymous stories in the Bible. She is in good company with the scores of other "players to be named later" in salvation history. The one thing they have in common is this: we don't know their names, but we know they were all changed by a powerful encounter with God. Why incorporate their stories in the Bible? If these individuals are not "important" enough to be remembered by name, why are they even included? I believe there are some very significant reasons these stories made it into our Holy Bible, even though the names of the individuals in them did not.

1. *They are included to show that every life, no matter how small, has significance to God.* Jesus knew the woman in this story, and he cared about her intimately whether or not anyone else there did. That is the case with us as well.
2. *They are included so that we can learn from the individuals' struggles and triumphs.* This woman's very public humiliation is part of history for all to read. But so is her very public redemption and the way Jesus loved her and treated her. Our own struggles, when redeemed by Christ, can become great gifts to others who learn from them.
3. *They are included to remind us that God is actually the main character in our stories, and it's God's name that should be lifted up, not ours.* One of the mistakes we often make is to believe that life is about us. Actually, this mistake is the root of all sin: placing ourselves at the center of the universe, where God belongs. We are all playing supporting roles in God's story. God is bigger than any of our individual stories.
4. *Maybe their names are left out so that we can put our own names "in the blank," so to speak, as we read their stories.* The anonymous stories of Scripture aren't meant to be fairy tales for our entertainment; they are each meant to teach us something that we can apply to our own lives.

I'm so thankful that this woman's story is included in God's Word! She may have been unnamed, but she was not unknown. Jesus knew her, and he loved her. He knows and loves you, too. If you ever feel a little anonymous, unremarkable, unnoticed, know that God notices your every joy and every concern. God is specifically concerned with the specifics of your life. Before you were born, God saw you. Before anyone spoke your name, God knew you. According to God, you are fearfully and wonderfully made. Yours is a story he cherishes.

Jesus' Next Move

Jesus was confronted in the Temple and asked to play judge in a very sensitive case. He had been put on the spot many times in his ministry, but this one was crucial. The decision Jesus was being forced to make was, on the surface, a decision about the sentencing of a woman caught breaking her marriage covenant. Her destiny was in his hands. And as we've seen, the decision he would make also would determine his own fate.

A decision to uphold the law of Moses would have half the crowd cheering and marching out into the street, filling their pockets with stones to begin an execution. But the Roman authorities, already leery of this man who could draw a crowd with his borderline revolutionary teaching, would most likely retaliate. A decision to have mercy and pardon her would have some in the crowd admiring his compassion, but the Pharisees would declare that he didn't really follow the laws of the Torah and wasn't a true man of God.

Rock. Hard place. Jesus in between.

You can bet that the crowd got quiet as they waited for Jesus' decision. The accusers who had dragged the woman before Jesus fell silent as they waited to see what he would do. One particular person listened with a special intensity, straining to hear the words that would come from this man's lips. Although a group of men had dragged her into this predicament, it was now just one man who would determine whether she lived or died. All eyes were on Jesus. But Jesus wasn't looking back at any of them. He was looking at the ground. And while they watched, "Jesus bent down and wrote with his finger on the ground" (John 8:6). This made them all even more curious. What was he writing? The text doesn't tell us.

The Greek verb used for write is *kategraphen*—indicating more than just doodling or drawing. It specifies that Jesus was writing words. Scholars who have studied this text have guessed, discussed, and guessed some more about what Jesus was writing on the ground.

Maybe Jesus was writing out a list of commandments or the sins of her accusers—so that they would recognize that none of them was above reproach. Maybe Jesus was writing out all the names of the men there who were also guilty of adultery. One particular guess I like is that Jesus might have been writing her name. He might have been humanizing this unknown woman, the one they had reduced to her sin, the one who was a pawn in their plot, the one whose life was at risk because they dragged her into the Temple to her own death-sentence trial.

If Jesus was writing her identity in the sand that day, those men accusing her would have had a hard time seeing her as an unnamed object. The one who created her and loved her was naming her before them to say, "This is not a mere creature. She is more than her sin. She is more than her mistakes. She has a name."

After all of the scholarship and study and discussion of what Jesus might have written that day, all we have are just good guesses. We'll never know what he wrote. We will come back to Jesus' statement to the woman's accusers in a moment. For now, I want to draw your attention to the fact that Jesus wrote not only once but twice in this story. The second time, after Jesus diffused the conflict, he wrote while her accusers trickled away, and he stopped only after they all left.

Why all this writing in the dirt? Why does the Gospel of John even include this detail in the story if it would just leave us with more questions than answers? It's interesting that this is the only time in the Gospels we're ever told Jesus wrote anything. We don't have a record of him writing a book or a letter or even his name. Outside of the Gospel stories, though, we do have images of God writing, inscribing things for us to remember through history. If we look at those other times God wrote, we might have some clues of the purpose of Jesus' writing in this story. We might be able to match the handwriting of God with the actions of Jesus in this story to find out more about what was going on.

First, there are the Ten Commandments. They were the ultimate standard for those who followed the law of Moses.

And let's not forget that one of those commandments was "You shall not commit adultery" (Exodus 20:14), the one that the accusers were supposedly so incensed that this woman had broken. That law was written in the first place by the very finger of God on stone tablets. That finger was now before them wearing human flesh and tracing in the dirt.

Another time the Bible speaks of God writing is in the book of Jeremiah (31:33). This time the law God promised to write wouldn't be inscribed on stone tablets or even a dirt floor:

> *But this is the covenant that I will make with*
> *the house of Israel after those days, says the*
> *Lord: I will put my law within them, and I*
> *will write it on their hearts; and I will be their*
> *God, and they shall be my people.*

God wants us to know that these laws we've been given aren't just for external consideration. He doesn't want us to keep the commands out of duty or obligation but because the desire to obey is written on our hearts out of love for God. God doesn't want us to use the law as a weapon of judgment, raising it over our heads like a stone to throw and hurt people when they break it. God's hope is that God's desires would become our desires. God wants not just a set of rules but a relationship.

In the story of the woman dragged before Jesus for judgment, the men who hauled her there against her will were guilty of a different kind of sin. They were worshiping an idol: the law itself. They cared far more about the law than they did about a relationship with the God behind it. They wanted to use the law to prove they were more holy than those around them. They were more concerned with the law God wrote than the people God loved.

In the telling of this story of the unnamed woman, the Gospel writer never questions that she was guilty of the sin of which she was accused. But just as guilty as the one who was breaking the law were the ones who were using the law to break her. As Jesus stooped and wrote on the ground that day, his message—whatever he might have written—somehow sunk deeper than just the dirt in which he wrote. It cut straight to the hearts of those who were watching and listening.

Finally, the men who had wielded the law like a weapon, both against the woman and against Jesus, were redirected to look within their own hearts. They stopped looking at her, or at Jesus, and started looking at themselves. And they gave up their quest and began, one by one, to walk away.

God wants our obedience, but even more than that, God wants our hearts—hearts that love God deeply and passionately, longing to spend time with God and to share the joy of our love with others.

God wants our obedience, but even more than that, God wants our hearts—hearts that love God deeply and passionately, longing to spend time with God and to share the joy of our love with others. If you sometimes feel that you've been following God out of obligation or duty, or that the joy of knowing God has dimmed, you're not alone. All of us have ups and downs in our relationship with God. But you can know today without a doubt that God loves you deeply and personally, that you matter. The God who created you and knows you through and through longs to write God's own love for you on your heart.

What Is in Your Heart?

The unnamed woman who was dragged into the Temple that day with Jesus was put in that precarious position not by troublemakers off the street but by religious insiders. When she was at her most vulnerable, it was followers of God who wounded her with words and actions of judgment. In their effort to take care that God's laws were followed, they had forgotten to take care not to hurt God's children.

Jesus was a man of few words in this story. Many rabbis might have taken the opportunity to give a treatise on the laws. Rabbis (both past and present) have filled whole books with teachings expounding on just one law. Jesus could have given a lengthy lecture, either to the accusers or to the accused. He chose, instead, to speak only two brief responses.

> *"Let anyone among you who is without sin be the first to throw a stone at her."*
>
> *(John 8:7)*

The accusers in this story were on the attack, advancing in their moral assault of this woman and closing in on Jesus with an ethical trap, but with just one sentence Jesus stopped them in their tracks. Instead of looking at the sins of others, he told them to take a look inside themselves. The question was not *What sin do you find in her?* but *What sin do you find in your own heart?*

When these men, so bold in their accusations, turned their judging eyes on themselves, they became all too aware that none of them (and none of us, for that matter) lives up to the standard of sinlessness Jesus was holding up here. The only one in that crowd who was without sin was the one offering that challenge, and he wasn't picking up any stones.

Jesus didn't condemn the sinner standing before him. He didn't even condemn the other sinners standing there. He had patience and compassion for both the accused and her accusers. "He who is without sin among you, let him throw the first stone at her" (John 8:7 WEB). I don't have statistics to prove it, but it's my bet that this is one of the most well-known verses in the Bible. I've even heard it quoted by people who don't know much about the Bible at all. They use it to defend themselves when they feel someone is judging them. I'm afraid they also quote it because they feel they have to defend themselves against Christians.

Though we don't pick up rocks to throw at people who have done wrong, we do hurl critical words. We fling disapproving looks. We lob rumors and gossip, even when they are disguised as concern or even as prayer requests.

When we talk about sin but don't want to sound judgmental, we often use the phrase "Love the sinner, hate the sin." That phrase is filled with good intentions, but it's still a symptom of our outward focus when it comes to sin. How often have you heard anyone say, "God hates sin. And God hates *my* sin! He hates my greed, my selfishness, my lust, my unforgiveness, my jealousy, my critical nature"?

The story of the unnamed woman shows us that God does want us to be on the lookout for sin, but the place God wants us to look is within ourselves. When we do, we will always find room for improvement. It also shows us how to look within the heart of God and find compassion and grace. This helps us keep from beating ourselves up about our past mistakes.

The intersection of those two hearts laid bare—our own heart marred by sin and the heart of Jesus, sinless and ready to forgive—is a beautiful place. Honesty about our own need for God's powerful and undeserved grace is the only thing that will bring us to confession, which pushes out sin and brings about a vacuum to be filled with forgiveness.

If we suppress the temptation to keep score in other people's lives long enough to look carefully at our own, we will find a record that is far from perfect. But the good news is that the one sinless heart in the crowd, the heart of Christ, is not one that throws stones at our sin.

When Jesus asked for the person without sin in the crowd of accusers to identify himself, no hand went up. That's still true today, isn't it? You and I both know that if we suppress the temptation to keep score in other people's lives long enough to look carefully at our own, we will find a record that is far from perfect. But the good news is that the one sinless heart in the crowd, the heart of Christ, is not one that throws stones at our sin. While others hurl judgment, Christ offers grace. If you'll let that simple truth sink in, it will dramatically change the way you see others—and yourself.

Jesus' Instructions

The unnamed woman had been vindicated against her enemies. The men who seemed so powerful and angry slunk away, licking the wounds of their own sin. What a great ending— except for one thing. The woman was still waiting on Jesus. He had said what he needed to say as a closing argument to her accusers, but she was still waiting on a verdict. She wanted to know: *What does he have to say to me?* This teacher had told those gathered to look into their own hearts to see if they were sinless. Clearly, she was not. So what would he have to say to her?

In that moment, Jesus offered her release and responsibility. His statements strike such a delicate balance. First he forgave her; then he set her on a new course in life. He transformed her story, giving her freedom from the past and a new path for the future, all in just two short phrases:

When Jesus had raised Himself up and saw no one but the woman, He said to her, "Woman, where are those accusers of yours? Has no one condemned you?"

She said, "No one, Lord."

And Jesus said to her, "Neither do I condemn you; go and sin no more."
(John 8:10-11 NKJV)

If Jesus had left her with that first statement, "Neither do I condemn you," she would have walked away free, but she might have walked right back into her life of sin. Yet he didn't stop there. Instead, he gave her a gentle command: "Go and sin no more" (John 8:11 NKJV). That phrase isn't quoted nearly as often as the verse we looked at earlier: "Let anyone among you who is without sin be the first to throw a stone at her" (John 8:7). It's a lot less popular—harder to say and harder to swallow. It says to us, *When you look inside and recognize your own sin, you need to do something about it.*

Jesus could have comforted her with a "There, there" and sent her on her way. He could have said, "Go, and be yourself; you're OK just the way you are"; "Go, and continue your relationship—you can't help who you love. All love is OK in my eyes"; "Go and enjoy yourself, you deserve to have a little fun." Instead, he said: "Go and sin no more" (John 8:11 NKJV).

"Sin no more" means God wants a better life for us than the one we've been leading. It means we have the responsibility to deal with our own impulses, desires, and temptations. It means not only that Jesus wants to forgive us and set us free from our pasts but also that he wants that freedom to stretch into our futures as well. He doesn't want us to continue on the same path and be damaged by the same mistakes over and over again. He wants to eradicate sin from its iron grip on our lives. God enters our messy first-draft lives, but he also longs to give us the gift of a rewrite that turns our future into a masterpiece.

Why does God want to free us from sin? Because of his love for us. Just like a parent trying to protect children from choices that can hurt them, God will do anything to protect us from the damaging presence of sin in our lives. Because sin hurts us so badly, it is God's enemy. And that is good news for us.

Listen Up

Just like each of us, the woman caught in adultery was a child of God. Jesus loved her and wanted for her a life of wholeness—one she could be proud of. He wanted to protect her from the damage her accusers were trying to inflict, but he also wanted to stop the damage she was inflicting on herself.

Not only did this woman experience the compassion and comfort of Jesus; she experienced conviction as well. Conviction is recognition of your own sin, and it humbles you and moves you to change. Let's talk a little more about the word *conviction*, because often when we first experience the awareness of our own sin, we have trouble distinguishing conviction from something else: condemnation.

Conviction is the internalized voice of God, affirming our worth, gently calling us to a life better than our own impulses and offering us a chance to change. *Condemnation* is the internalized voices of others that have called us broken and worthless. It calls out the nicknames of our past based on our worst actions and impulses. It's a voice that condemns us to fail over and over again.

Conviction is an awareness that offers us a chance to change with God's help. Condemnation is a voice that says: you will never change. One is the voice of God. The other is never, ever the voice of God.

If you're hearing the voice of condemnation, the one that tells you you'll never be good enough, never change, never be acceptable to God, then it's time to tell it to *shut up!* Because this voice, which often masquerades as the voice of God, is an insidious trick. It drives you farther from God who offers forgiveness for free when we simply recognize our need for God.

But if you're hearing a voice of conviction, the one that gently corrects, invites you to change, and whispers that there's a path better than the one you're headed down, then continue to *listen up.* God doesn't point out sin because God is against you. God is for you and wants to help you change for the better.

There is no place for the voice of condemnation in a Christian's life. The Bible is clear on that point. The Son of God did not come into this world to condemn: "Therefore, there is now no condemnation for those who are in Christ Jesus" (Romans 8:1 NIV). God doesn't want us to stay captive to our sin, which separates us from God, but neither does God want us captive to a voice that tells us we don't deserve God's forgiveness and grace—or that we're not capable of being better than we have been in the past. That voice also separates us from God, and it is a lie.

When we look at Jesus' interaction with the woman caught in adultery, we don't find even a hint of condemnation. What we do find is an offer to change with his help, an offer at a life that won't keep damaging her, an offer to stop being branded by her past. Jesus didn't want her to be known for the rest of her life as the woman caught in adultery. He wanted to free her from the voice of condemnation and from the path that had held her captive in the past.

I've always felt a little frustrated that, as in many other narratives of Jesus' encounters in Scripture, we don't know the end of this woman's story. We don't know if she took Jesus up on his offer of a new life. Sometimes, though, I think stories like this are open-ended so that we can imagine the ending ourselves. Envisioning her ending helps us, in a way, ask what we want our own endings to be.

I wonder if you've ever felt the crushing weight of condemnation in your own life. Have you ever felt stuck in a rut of your own behavior or trapped by the mistakes of your past? The story of the unnamed woman is a gift for those of us who long to lead different lives with God's help. It unveils the beautiful balance Jesus achieves between releasing us from condemnation and offering us responsibility and freedom to choose a different future. That offer stands open for you today!

CLOSING THOUGHTS

When Jesus was eight days old, his parents took him to his first religious ceremony, the first of many that he would attend in his lifetime as an observant Jew. But this one was personal. This is where he received his name. The mortality rate for infants in childbirth and shortly after was so great that parents held off giving their boy babies an official name until their circumcision ceremony on their eighth day.

When it came time for Mary and Joseph to announce their tiny baby's name before God and everyone at this ceremony, the name they spoke was probably a shock to many. "His name is *Jesus*."

To those in attendance, this would have been surprising because traditionally firstborn sons were named after their fathers. One reason we know about this custom is that Jesus' slightly older cousin John was also given a surprising name. When we read the story of Jesus' naming, we have the benefit of two pieces of information that most people who were there that day probably did not know. First, we know that Jesus' name was decided before his birth or circumcision day and was not chosen by his parents. Second, we know that despite what people might have expected, Jesus *was* given a first name that reflected his father's identity. It wasn't the name of his earthly adopted father, Joseph, but a name that reflected the character of his Father in heaven.

In Numbers 13, God commanded Moses to send twelve spies into the land of Canaan to see how fruitful it was and how dangerous it might be for God's people to move into. One man was chosen from each of the twelve tribes. In Numbers 13:8 we learn the identity of the spy from the tribe of Ephraim: "Hoshea son of Nun." Only just a few verses later, we read that Hoshea's name was changed—a practice that by now should not surprise us! Just a few verses after he is first mentioned, he is Hoshea no more.

This time it's not God who renames someone but a leader, a mentor in faith. Hoshea's name originally meant "salvation," but *Joshua,* tweaked by the addition of a new first letter, means "The Lord is salvation" or "God saves." That new letter, *yod,* was meant to point to the name of God revealed to Moses at the burning bush: Jehovah—the name we translate "I am." By adding that letter it made Hoshea's name—"The desire for salvation or rescue"—a reality. By speaking Joshua's new name, Moses was actually naming aloud the one responsible for his people's rescue: Jehovah. Once God's people had been so afraid to pronounce that name that they deliberately inserted the wrong consonants for fear that someone would try to say the name of God aloud and by doing so commit blasphemy and incur judgment. Now they were trying to call on that name when they knew they needed saving help, salvation, the most.

As those spies went on their dangerous mission, this one man, Joshua, would prove to be different than the majority of his peers. It's possible that his new name gave him the confidence and insight to see God's hand in every situation, even as dangerous as they found that new land to be. He and one other man, Caleb, would not be afraid of the overwhelming power they found there but would declare that God could give the people victory—that God was powerful enough to save in any situation, just as Joshua's new name announced.

Joshua was right about God's ability to save the people and bring them victoriously into the Promised Land. He became a great leader of God's people, one who went down in history as trusting that "God saves," just as his name proclaimed.

When Mary and Joseph were called on to name their baby boy, the name they spoke over him, the name an angel commanded each of them to give him, was Joshua. *God saves.* The Hebrew name *Joshua* in our Greek translations of the New Testament becomes *Iésous*, or *Jesus.* Jesus' first name was Joshua.

In the moment that he received the name Jesus, God the Son became the namesake of God the Father. His name was an echo of the "I am" (Jehovah) given at the burning bush, that first invitation for God's people to know God's name.

The truly shocking thing that happened that day is not that Jesus wasn't named Joseph Jr.; it's that God offered humanity a chance to be on a first-name basis with God! Jesus, "God saves," is his name and job description all rolled into one. And Jesus fulfilled his name on the cross and through his resurrection when he proved once and for all that God indeed saves.

Through God's Son, Jesus, we have the opportunity to approach God on a first-name basis. That ultimate revelation of who God is and how close to us God desires to be alters our understanding of God in a spectacular way. What a change from God's people being afraid even to address God out loud! "Call me Jesus." Aren't you thankful that God invites us to that kind of closeness? God rewrote the story of history to mean that he could be close to his people, with no sin or shame in between. At just the parts that should have been hardest for us, he wrote his own name to take the brunt of the suffering and shame. God literally edited history so that we could have life and have it abundantly with him.

Through Jesus, we have an intimate relationship with God, the Creator and finisher of our stories. If your story right now is not living up to the version that God wants to write in your life, invite God to take the pen and transform your story. God has the power, creativity, love, mercy, and grace to take your current circumstances and write a beautiful story of redemption. I hope you'll invite God to rewrite your story today. I'm so grateful for lives like the ones we've explored together that remind us that God has the power to change our stories—and even our names—when we need it most!

NOTE

1. Chaya Babu, "285 Indian girls shed 'unwanted' names,"
   Yahoo! News, October 22, 2011, http://news.yahoo.
   com/285-indian-girls-shed-unwanted-names-122551876
   .html, accessed November 5, 2016.